WORD IS OUT

Arsenal Pulp Press | Vancouver

WORD IS OUT

STORIES OF SOME OF OUR LIVES

A Queer Film Classic

Greg Youmans

ARSENAL PULP PRESS
211 East Georgia Street, Suite 101
Vancouver, BC V6A 1Z6 Canada
arsenalpulp.com

Efforts have been made to locate copyright holders of source material wherever possible. The publisher welcomes hearing from any copyright holders of material used in this book who have not been contacted.

Queer Film Classics series editors: Matthew Hays and Thomas Waugh

Cover and text design by Shyla Seller
Edited for the press by Lindsey Hunnewell and Susan Safyan
All film stills (except where indicated) courtesy of the San Francisco Public Library, Mariposa Film Group and Milliarium Films
Photograph of the author by Chris Vargas; photograph on page 5 by Greg Youmans

Printed and bound in Canada

CANADIAN CATALOGUING IN PUBLICATION DATA

Library and Archives Canada Cataloguing in Publication

Youmans, Greg, 1977-
    Word is out / Greg Youmans.

(A queer film classic)
Includes bibliographical references and index.
Issued also in electronic format.
ISBN 978-1-55152-420-7

    1. Word is out (Motion picture). 2. Mariposa Film
Group—Criticism and interpretation. I. Title.
II. Series: Queer film classics

HQ75.2.Y68 2011   306.76'6092273   C2011-906394-8

For Sally and Chris

CONTENTS

ACKNOWLEDGMENTS

I have been thinking about *Word Is Out* for a long time, and I have many, many people to thank. Unfortunately, in such a short book, I cannot justify going on and on about each person. I promise that one day soon I will write a longer book and gush about everyone.

I began thinking about the film when I was a graduate student in the History of Consciousness program at the University of California, Santa Cruz. Among the people who shaped my early thinking are Teresa de Lauretis and Barbara Epstein, as well as my main dissertation advisers: Angela Davis, Carla Freccero, Peter Limbrick, and the affable Canadian outsider Thomas Waugh.

Lucas Hilderbrand and Nguyen Tan Hoang read my manuscript when it was at a particularly rough, early stage, and they gave me invaluable feedback and guidance. Series editors Matthew Hays and Thomas Waugh similarly worked wonders at the next stage. I am grateful to Tom, Matt, and everyone at Arsenal Pulp Press for making this book-length study of *Word Is Out* possible. Thank you in particular to Lindsey Hunnewell, Susan Safyan, and Shyla Seller for taking the manuscript through the final stages of revisions and layout.

The book is made richer because so many people involved with the film were willing to talk candidly with me about their experiences. I spoke in person with five of the film's six filmmakers, and I also met or corresponded with a number of people who appear in the film. More than anyone else, Veronica Selver graciously put up with my repeated emails and questions about the film. A key moment in the project occurred on a magical day in spring 2009 when my boyfriend and I drove up to Willits, California, to meet with Sally Gearhart. The dedication photograph is taken from that afternoon. For me, the photograph represents the type of exchange across queer generations, experiences, and worldviews that *Word Is Out* inspires and that I hope this book continues.

The one filmmaker whom I was not able to interview for this project was Peter Adair, who died in 1996. Thankfully, his voice lives on not only in his films, but also in the bountiful Peter Adair Papers at the San Francisco Public Library. Tim Wilson, Susan Goldstein, and the rest of the staff at the library's History Center were incredibly kind and helpful during my many visits. I am likewise grateful to Rebekah Kim at the GLBT Historical Society for her assistance at various stages of the project. John Carlson at City College of San Francisco made it possible for me to view a 16mm print of the educational version of *Word Is Out* after I had bounced from institution to institution in search of a working projector. Small world: when we got the film up and running, he remembered having worked on it as a colorist at Monaco Labs in the late 1970s. I am grateful to Dennis Doros of

Milestone Films and everyone else who agreed to let me reproduce stills and photographs for this book.

I live with three incredible housemates who I thank for their kindness and patience as I worked on the manuscript. Kentaro Kaneko graciously came through with vital tech support when my laptop died in the eleventh hour. Our irrepressible feline companion Holiday always had something to say about the book, which I interpreted as praise or criticism depending on my mood. And in his endless good spirit, Chris Vargas solidified his standing as the love of my life.

Lastly, Marcos Becquer was a colleague and friend in the History of Consciousness program who had a profound, early influence on my thinking about both queer film and the gay 1970s. Marcos and I often disagreed about things. In passionate exchanges, he challenged my ideas time and again, always helping to make my thinking more nuanced and more just. Marcos died suddenly and tragically as I was finishing my first draft of this manuscript, and I did not have a chance to share my most recent ideas about *Word Is Out* with him. This book, like its author, suffers because of his loss.

[handwritten: Book published 2011]

SYNOPSIS AND CAST OF CHARACTERS

Word Is Out: Stories of Some of Our Lives is a documentary made up of interwoven interviews with more than twenty lesbians and gay men. The onscreen subjects recount anecdotes from their lives and speak to a range of topics relating to gay and lesbian identity. After a brief opening sequence, the film unfolds in three parts, each introduced by a title card: "Part One: The Early Years," "Part Two: Growing Up," and "Part Three: From Now On." The interview material is broken up by short vérité sequences involving the interview subjects as well as musical interludes featuring the gay male group Buena Vista and feminist singer-songwriter Trish Nugent.

[handwritten: >20 people]

The chapter "N Is for Narrative" presents a discussion of the rhetorical and thematic design of the film. What follows is a list of the film's main interview subjects, beginning with the people introduced in Part One. Intended as an aid in navigating the book, the list provides brief biographical notes describing *who the subjects were at the time the film was made*. It also includes dates of birth and death for the participants who have since passed away.[1]

---

1. A number of sources were used to construct this list, including N. Adair and C. Adair (1978) and an untitled promotional document in the Adair Papers (box 33, folder 26) that presents photographs and descriptive blurbs for the film's main subjects.

Part One:

Pat Bond (1925–1990): Longtime resident of San
Francisco, performer and comedienne, served as a nurse
in the US Women's Army Corps during World War II.

John Burnside (1916–2008): Living in New Mexico, lover
of Harry Hay, inventor of various kaleidoscopic optical
devices, soon to be a founding member of the Radical
Faeries.

Bernice "Whitey" Fladden: Living in the country in
Northern California, formerly a bartender at the San
Francisco lesbian bar Maud's.

Sally Gearhart: San Francisco State University speech
professor, feminist activist and theorist, and writer of
lesbian-separatist science fiction.

Elsa Gidlow (1898–1986): Septuagenarian writer,
sometimes known as "the poet of Druid Heights" in
reference to the artists' community where she lived in
Marin County (just north of San Francisco).

Donald Hackett (1944–1995): Recently unemployed truck
driver, living in Philadelphia.

Roger Harkenrider (known today as Tom Fitzpatrick):
Boston actor and the film's spokesperson for the
"weirdos" and "faggots" of the world.

Harry Hay (1912–2002): Living in New Mexico, lover of
John Burnside, theorist of gay male sexuality and identity,
former Communist organizer, founder in the early 1950s

of the Mattachine Society, soon to be a founding member of the Radical Faeries.

Pam Jackson: Waitress and mother, separated from her two sons in a custody dispute, living with Rusty Millington and Millington's four children in San Mateo, California.

George Mendenhall (1930–1994): San Francisco factory worker and gay activist journalist.

Rusty Millington: Working-class butch lesbian, living with her four children and Pam Jackson in San Mateo.

Mark Pinney: New York businessman and the film's spokesperson for gay conservatives.

Rick Stokes: Activist lawyer, formerly a co-owner of the Ritch Street Health Club (a gay men's bathhouse in San Francisco), campaigned against Harvey Milk for San Francisco City Supervisor in 1977.

Part Two:

Nadine Armijo (1940–1987): Currently unemployed, living in a house in New Mexico with her lover, Rosa Montoya.

Dennis Chiu: Recent graduate of Amherst College, living in San Francisco.

Cynthia Gair: Lesbian-feminist activist living in Washington DC, cofounder with Helaine Harris of Women in Distribution (WinD), an organization that distributed books and periodicals produced by the women's movement.

Nathaniel "Nick" Dorsky: Renowned San Francisco-based experimental filmmaker.

David Gillon: Recent graduate of the University of Massachusetts where he studied radio broadcasting.

Freddy Gray: Gay father, bassist for the San Francisco musical group Buena Vista, lover of filmmaker Andrew Brown.

Linda Marco: Former homecoming queen and member of Triangle Area Lesbian Feminists (TALF) in North Carolina.

Tede Mathews (1951–1993): San Francisco-based poet and male feminist, the film's spokesperson for male androgyny and gender radicalism.

Michael Mintz (1955–1995): Student and athlete at Princeton University.

Betty Powell (now Achebe Powell): Professor in the school of education at Brooklyn College, co-chairperson of the Board of Directors of the National Gay Task Force, involved with a number of other activist groups of the 1970s including the National Black Feminist Organization and Salsa Soul Sisters.

Ann Samsell: North Carolina-based veterinarian and a member of TALF along with Linda Marco.

In addition to these main participants, a few other people appear and are interviewed on camera, most notably: Nadine Armijo's lover Rosa Montoya, Michael Mintz's lover Earl Carter, and Rick Stokes' lover David Clayton.

Handwritten at top: Word Is Out: Coming out
Momentum for social progress
what word is out?

CREDITS

Word Is Out: Stories of Some of Our Lives
1978, USA, English
132 min (prerelease length: 142 min)
Color, Sound, 35mm (blown up from 16mm), 1.33:1

A film by the Mariposa Film Group: Nancy Adair, Peter Adair, Andrew Brown, Rob Epstein, Lucy Massie Phenix, and Veronica Selver
Producer: Peter Adair
Camera, sound, interviews, and editing: Nancy Adair, Peter Adair, Andrew Brown, Rob Epstein, Lucy Massie Phenix, and Veronica Selver
Women's Music composed and performed by Trish Nugent with Marcia Bauman, Kristen Brooks, Robin Osborne, and Carol Vendrillo
Men's Music performed by Buena Vista: Dickie Dworkin, Michael Gomes, Freddy Gray, Terry Hutchison, Joe Nathan Johnson, Jon Raskin, and Kenny Ross, with Donn Tatum

The film premiered on December 1, 1977, at the Castro Theater in San Francisco, followed by a short theatrical run in the same city. That winter the Mariposa Film Group cut ten minutes from the film, and the final version played in

Handwritten in right margin: Film 1977

theaters across the US and Canada throughout 1978. *Word Is Out* first appeared on public television in October 1978.

The film was preserved as part of the Outfest Legacy Project for LGBT Film Preservation and restored by the UCLA Film & Television Archive, in collaboration with the Mariposa Film Group and the James C. Hormel Gay & Lesbian Center of the San Francisco Public Library. The preservation and restoration were funded by the David Bohnett Foundation with additional support from the Andrew J. Kuehn, Jr. Foundation and members of Outfest. Restorationist: Ross Lipman. The restored film premiered in 2008.

A thirtieth-anniversary DVD of *Word Is Out* was released in 2010 by Milliarium Zero, a sister company of Milestone Films. DVD produced by Veronica Selver and Janet Cole. Executive producer: David Bohnett.

INTRODUCTION

I was born in 1977, the year that *Word Is Out* premiered. I was well into my twenties when I first saw the film, and I found it difficult to grasp its historical significance. As I imagine is the case with others who came of age in and after the mid-1990s, I had trouble understanding how so pleasant an image of ordinary people could have been groundbreaking or how it could have functioned as a powerful political tool. *Word Is Out* is deceptively simple. As a documentary comprised of talking-head interviews about purportedly universal gay and lesbian experiences, it can pass as formless, apolitical, and timeless. Moreover, because the world it presents is now the norm for a number of lesbians and gay men—who today live openly gay lives as integrated members of mainstream society—it is difficult to appreciate *Word Is Out* as an activist film (i.e., a film that helped to make this cultural shift a reality) rather than as a documentary reflection of a truth that already existed.

The story of *Word Is Out* is the story of many people coming together and putting aside their differences of ideology and experience to make the film. When Peter Adair (1943–1996), the film's creator and producer, initially proposed the project in 1974, no major foundations would support it. For the next four years, he spearheaded an exhausting but fruitful campaign to raise funds directly from lesbians and gay

FIGURE 1. The Mariposa Film Group, from left to right: Rob Epstein, Veronica Selver, Peter Adair, Lucy Massie Phenix, Andrew Brown, and Nancy Adair. Photograph by Janet Cole. Courtesy of the San Francisco Public Library, the Mariposa Film Group, and Milliarium Films. Photograph by Janet Cole.

men, largely through a number of community screenings of the work in progress. Roughly $200,000 US—four-fifths of the film's quarter-million-dollar budget—came from individual donations, usually at around $1,000 each. The other $50,000 was raised through the advance sale of the television rights to the New York PBS affiliate WNET.

Grassroots funding [handwritten margin note]

The making of the film likewise involved a host of people. The filmmakers conducted video pre-interviews with more than 140 lesbians and gay men, from whom they selected more than twenty-five to re-interview on celluloid. Adair initially teamed up with his sister Nancy Adair (b. 1947) and then, throughout 1976 and 1977, with four other filmmakers: Andrew Brown (b. 1947), Rob Epstein (b. 1955), Lucy Massie Phenix (b. 1942), and Veronica Selver (b. 1944). Together they formed the Mariposa Film Group, which, like the bulk of the film's funders and interview subjects, was based in the San Francisco Bay Area.

Bay Area [handwritten margin note]

The many people who supported and participated in *Word Is Out* presented a united front: they collaborated on a distilled positive image of gay men and lesbians, which they then sent forth to change the hearts and minds of both straight people and closeted gay people. There were certainly non-fiction films by gay people about gay people before *Word Is Out*, but none achieved its comprehensiveness—i.e., its national scope, its balanced presentation of both men and women—or its reach. The film screened theatrically across the country, which was no small feat for a feature documentary. Perhaps more importantly, it was broadcast nationally on public television in October 1978, thereby reaching viewers who were not able or inclined to see it in an urban theater.

Like the film itself, this account of its production history has so far presented an image of gay and lesbian diversity that is not fractured by difference. However, anyone who spends time in the Peter Adair Papers at the San Francisco Public Library soon discovers that many currents move beneath the film's placid surface. The Adair collection includes the video pre-interviews that the filmmakers conducted with subjects who were not selected for the final cast. One could readily imagine many of these people appearing in *Word Is Out*, but others seem to be less likely fits: prostitutes, hippie commune folk, and political radicals (or at least radicals who seem unwilling to put on "positive-image" drag for the cause). The archive also houses handwritten notes, including things jotted on interview transcripts and on various drafts of the book that accompanied the film.[2] These notes convey the filmmakers' conflicting opinions as to who should appear in the final film and which parts of their testimony should

specific editorial cuts - thematic

---

2. The accompanying book was published in 1978 and is edited by Nancy Adair and Casey Adair (Peter and Nancy's mother). Also called *Word Is Out: Stories of Some of Our Lives*, the book compiles the transcripts of the full celluloid interviews with the subjects who appear in the film. It also features Nancy Adair's lengthy account of the film's making.

be included. By all accounts, attendees of the community pre-screenings likewise voiced conflicting opinions as to who and what the film should include. There were conflicts between lesbians and gay men, clashes between separatists and assimilationists, and interrogations of the film's breadth and balance in terms of gender, class, and race. There were also disagreements over whether the film should pay more or less attention to particular issues and representations, such as gay male effeminacy, clone masculinity, drag, lesbian separatism, monogamy, couples, and families.[3] However successful the film is at presenting an image of harmony, its production history created forums in which queer people passed judgment and gave voice to their prejudices about other queer people who were different from themselves. For at least one of the film's makers, Andrew Brown, the experience was traumatic, and he distanced himself from the project for many years after it was released.[4]

When the film premiered, most reviewers in the main-

3. The community pre-screenings are discussed in N. Adair (1978), Mariposa Film Group (1978), and Waugh (1977). A few completed feedback forms are included in the Peter Adair Papers. The pre-screenings also came up in my interviews with the five surviving filmmakers. I do not want to overstate the amount of conflict that occurred at these screenings. They were also sites of positive feedback and encouragement, as the film's fundraising history attests.

4. Brown told me this during my interview with him on August 18, 2009.

Mainstream praise

stream press praised it. Reviews in the gay activist press and in leftist film journals tended to be more critical. To generalize, these reviews often involved gay film critics saying that they were deeply moved by the film but disturbed by its soft-pedaling of sex and politics and by its assimilationist ideological position. I like to picture these critics railing against the film's agenda with tears in their eyes. To generalize further, the film's journey in the 1970s—from the earliest community pre-screenings to late-run showings in theaters, on television, and at community events at the close of the decade—began with the filmmakers' navigation of entrenched conflicts between and among lesbians and gay men but ended with their arrival at a much less treacherous and divided landscape.

This journey from dissension to apparent consensus paralleled larger developments of the mid- to late-1970s. The year 1977 was a historical turning point when gay and lesbian politics were dramatically transformed by the rise of the Christian Right and a series of local gay-rights struggles that became national controversies. The most famous battles occurred around Anita Bryant's "Save Our Children" campaign to overturn an antidiscrimination ordinance in Dade County (Miami), Florida, and California State Senator John Briggs' Proposition 6 to outlaw gay teachers in public schools. These threats to gay rights prompted many lesbians and gay men to participate in activism for the first time; they spurred others into a political reawakening after

a mid-1970s slumber; and they absorbed still others into a
liberal political agenda after they had spent years criticizing
and practicing alternatives to liberalism. In the late 1970s
it became possible to talk about a unified "gay and lesbian
movement" for the first time, both because lesbians and
gay men were coming out of various separatisms to work
together politically and because activists could now claim
consensus: a national movement seemed to be forming with
a set, agreed-upon program of gay rights. It was in the midst
of this transformed context that *Word Is Out* appeared, in the
wake of the losing battle against Bryant and just as activists
were gearing up for the battle against Briggs.

Unified activism [margin annotation]

A main task of this book is to trace the course of this historical development and to understand the role that *Word Is
Out* played in it. I hope to make the film visible in its complexity as a work of cultural activism, perhaps especially for
those of us who were not there and who now exist on this
far side of the late 1970s when gay liberalism and a gay-
rights agenda again dominate and define the mainstream of
US LGBT politics. As a scholar, I initially turned to the late
1970s to find out how and why gay radicalism dissipated,
rather than to celebrate the ascendancy of gay liberalism.
Because of my investment in the comparatively oppositional cultural-feminist and gay-liberationist impulses of the
1970s, when I first wrote about *Word Is Out* a few years ago I
was almost uniformly critical of it—this despite a strong at-
tachment to many of the interview subjects (Pat Bond, Sally

Gearhart, Elsa Gidlow, and the list has only grown since), and despite having conducted interviews of my own with the five surviving filmmakers of the Mariposa Film Group. Like the time I spent with the Adair Papers, these interviews convinced me that the film and its history are irreducible to any one argument. Given the opportunity to write this book, I wanted to devise a structure that would allow for more richness and contradiction.

Word Is Out opens with a title card that reads "Conversations with 26 gay men and women." Yet, oddly, it is impossible to make the number of interview subjects who appear in the film add up to twenty-six. Because the film privileges both diversity and language, I had at first assumed the filmmakers chose the number because it is the number of letters in the alphabet. Perhaps the film was presenting itself as a cinematic alphabet-book of gay and lesbian life, a primer for those who were new to the people and their customs. However, when I ran this interpretation by some of the filmmakers, they expressed surprise and said that the idea had never occurred to them.[5] Nevertheless, the idea of writing

Handwritten margin note: Film - 26 ↓ Today's diversity?

---

5. At the beginning of parts One and Two of *Word Is Out*, the film presents a grid of names and still photographs of the interviewees, but only twenty-five people are introduced in this way. One of them, Trish Nugent, is never interviewed on film, though we do see and hear her sing. At the same time, a handful of people who are not introduced with names and still photographs appear and are interviewed in the film as either lovers or family members of

an alphabet-book of my own stayed with me. If I broke my discussion of the film up into multiple, differently themed segments, I might avoid reducing everything to one argument or to one political critique. I could be critical in one section and celebratory in another, or descriptive here and analytical there. I could let the sections speak dialectically with each other, and maybe open the book up to differently charted courses through the material. With excitement, I parsed the film into various topics: some broadly historical, some tightly biographical, some about the film's production history, some about its form, some about its representations of race and gender, and some about issues of historical memory and political legacy as we look back on the film from the present. And finally, because the film itself never adds up to twenty-six interviewees, no matter how you shake it, I took the liberty of only using twenty-five letters myself. For the life of me, I couldn't come up with a good "J."

Book-
25

---

the main participants. In the film's closing credits, the filmmakers express "special gratitude to the 28 people who trusted us to freeze a moment of their lives for this film."

A IS FOR ANITA *Bryant*

Word Is Out premiered at San Francisco's Castro Theater on December 1, 1977, as a benefit screening for gay-rights organizations. The event was specifically in support of the struggle against California's Proposition 6, also known as the Briggs Initiative. A conservative state senator with gubernatorial ambitions, John Briggs sought to capitalize on the voter turnout and national media attention of Anita Bryant's "Save Our Children" campaign in Dade County, Florida, earlier that year. Like Bryant, Briggs argued that openly gay teachers posed a moral and sexual threat to children.

[handwritten margin note: CA Prop 6: gay teachers]

Until 1977, gay rights had not been a particularly heated issue. Between 1972 and 1976, twenty-nine US cities and counties had quietly enacted laws and policies protecting gay men and lesbians from discrimination (Fejes 2008, 53). The Dade County Metro Commission was in the process of doing the same when Bryant caught wind of it. A devout Southern Baptist and mother of four, Bryant was also a national celebrity: a former beauty queen, popular gospel singer, bestselling author in religious markets, and the spokesperson for Florida Orange Juice. In this last capacity she entered homes across America each day with her phrase, "A day without orange juice is like a day without sunshine." Within a month of the Commission passing its anti-discrimination ordinance, her campaign gathered six times the necessary 10,000 signatures to bring the issue to public vote. When the citizens of Dade County voted, the ordinance went down in a landslide: forty-five percent of the electorate turned out, nearly seventy percent of them voting against gay rights (Clendinen and Nagourney 1999, 308).

The day of the defeat, June 7, 1977, would go down in infamy as "Orange Tuesday." Spontaneous protests erupted in cities across the nation. At these protests and others that year, a strange slogan appeared on signs and banners. The phrase "Thank You Anita!" called attention to the many ways that Bryant's campaign could be seen as a boon rather than a defeat for gays and lesbians. For one, her celebrity status and the polarization of values and opinions spawned by her campaign brought unprecedented mass-media visibility to the issue of gay rights. In the months leading up to the vote, many major print and television news sources gave time and space to the story. Certainly some of this coverage was hostile toward gays and lesbians, as was the rash of moral-panic news segments and TV movies on the topics of pedophile rings, teen prostitution, child pornography, and child sexual abuse—all of which had a disproportionate slant toward adult male relationships with boys (Jenkins 1998, 122). However, much of the coverage relating to the struggle against Bryant presented gays and lesbians as a legitimate minority engaged in a dignified struggle for civil rights against hysterical bigots. The fundamentalists' attack also drew many gay men and lesbians into activism for the first time. At the various

Media attention

31

Gay Pride and Gay Freedom Day parades and marches around the nation that year—which mark the late-June anniversary of the Stonewall Riots, and thus were scheduled only a few weeks after the June 7 vote—a new intensity was felt among the participants. Many turned out in New York City and San Francisco, as expected. However, according to *Time* magazine, "With record gay participation in Atlanta, Chicago, Los Angeles, San Diego, and Seattle as well, the weekend marked the biggest nationwide protest demonstration since the days of the antiwar movement."[6]

Bryant's campaign also helped to forge a coalition among lesbians and gay men, who had spent most of the decade organizing and socializing separately. This new coalition was enabled largely by the ease with which the religious Right collapsed the issues of abortion, the Equal Rights Amendment, lesbian child custody, pornography, and gay teachers into one unified assault on family values. A durable network of political organizations took shape as seasoned activists from the gay enclaves of New York City, Los Angeles, and San Francisco, as well as those working with the National Gay Task Force in Washington, DC, struggled to transport skills, money, and activist personnel to Miami. Over the next two years they would work to do the same in every other lo-

6. "The Band Gets Bigger," *Time*, July 11, 1977, 30. Pride celebrations the following year, in the midst of the battle against Briggs, would be even bigger.

cal arena engaged in a gay-rights struggle. The battle against
Bryant also included a famous demonstration of gay economic clout in the form of a national, and in some instances
international, orange juice boycott, which marked the movement's first major assertion of "economic citizenship" (Chasin 2000, 160–73). For many gay and lesbian activists, all of
these early-1977 developments seemed like good reasons to
thank Anita. At the same time, they struck others as evidence
of a much less positive development: the decisive shift and
consolidation of gay and lesbian politics into a rights-based
movement, invested in gaining access to US cultural and political institutions rather than transforming them.

OJ boycott

Access vs. transform

   In the new climate of mass-media scrutiny and Right
smear-campaigning, gay liberal activists felt themselves under intense pressure to present gay men and lesbians as a respectable group of people. In this regard, *Word Is Out* came
along in the nick of time. With its stigma-free presentation of
responsible gay citizens, the film seemed tailor-made for the
struggle against Briggs. In addition to the Castro premiere,
Word Is Out and its makers appeared at benefits for BACABI
(Bay Area Coalition Against the Briggs Initiative), the Gay
National Educational Switchboard, Save Our Human Rights,
and Gay Rights Advocates, among other groups. Unlike the
majority of the gay-liberal activist projects with which it was
mobilized, *Word Is Out* predated 1977 in its conception and
most of its production. Peter Adair came up with the basic
vision for the film as early as 1973, and judging by his 1974

Respectable

proposal, key elements of the final film were in place from the beginning: the reasoned tone, the presentation of a universal gay and lesbian experience, the investment in positive role models, and the promotion of inclusion and tolerance (P. Adair 1974). A few additions at the level of content were made in 1977: most notably the decision to include the interview with Sally Gearhart, as well as footage of Gearhart speaking at that summer's Gay Freedom Day parade in San Francisco (N. Adair 1978, 304).[7] Beyond this, the impact of the events of 1977 was felt mainly in the increased success the filmmakers had with fundraising and promotion that year, as well as, to some extent, in the film's positive reception and impressive crossover success upon release.[8] Although we cannot take the late-1970s rechanneling of US gay and lesbian activism as the determining factor behind the film's form and politics, this only encourages us to think about how the film actively shaped the historical events in which it participated, and how it contributed to the new understandings of gay and lesbian experience that were emerging at the time.

---

7. Nancy Adair's account of the film's making indicates that Dennis Chiu and Nathaniel Dorsky were also brought in at this late stage (1978, 306-07).

8. Michael Bronski argued at the time of the film's release that the "liberal anti-Bryant backlash" played a role in the many positive reviews of the film in the mainstream press, such as Janet Maslin's review in *The New York Times* (Bronski 1978; Maslin 1978).

B IS FOR BURDEN OF REPRESENTATION

On January 29, 1976, Peter Adair wrote a letter to Robert
Kotlowitz of WNET, the New York City public television
station. WNET had expressed interest in Adair's film project after seeing an early composite of video pre-interviews
(N. Adair 1978, 285). In the letter, Adair discusses how the
project has evolved from his original conception of it as a
short educational film intended for classroom use, which was
initially budgeted at $70,000 and featured only ten interview
subjects. He also discusses the heavy burden of representation that he now feels himself to be shouldering.

> My sister and I, after having done more than fifty
> video interviews, are becoming increasingly aware
> of the great responsibility we are taking on (whether
> we like it or not) by doing this film. Without trying
> to sound melodramatic, this movie has to make
> up (or at least begin to make up) for thousands of
> years of anonymity. Real homosexual culture has
> always had to remain invisible in Western society
> at least. This first exploration into who we are will
> be taken (again, whether we like it or not) by both
> gays and straights as the gospel truth. It is almost as
> if some documentary of an undiscovered tribe in the
> Amazon were made, everything in it would have to

Books belong to their readers

Definition – group vs. individual

be accepted as accurate simply because of the absence of any other material. But this documentary on Our Tribe is especially important because it will directly affect the tribe itself. This film will have impact on gay people (like it or not) in determining what we will be because it will be a first definition of who we are.[9]

No doubt in order to help sell his cause, Adair is a bit hyperbolic about the "anonymity" of gay and lesbian life in the 1970s and "the absence of any other material" representing this population. There were motion-picture portraits of gay men and lesbians before *Word Is Out*, as well as portrayals in other media forms like books and music. It is true, though, that until *Word Is Out* came along, virtually none of the moving-image records of gay and lesbian life reaching a wide audience were made by openly gay filmmakers. Mass-media portrayals of homosexuality were often stigmatizing and sensationalistic: journalistic or ethnographic accounts of a shadowy subculture. The film's working title, *Who Are We?*, indicates Adair's desire to push aside these distorted images and present a truer definition of gay and lesbian people.

Adair's auto-ethnographic framing of the film reflects his family and professional background. Peter and Nancy's father was visual anthropologist John Adair (1913–1997), whose most famous project involved teaching a group of Na-

9. This letter, along with other correspondence between Adair and WNET, can be found in the Adair Papers (box 33, folder 7).

FIGURE 2. During the opening sequence of *Word Is Out*, Betty Powell feels her own burden of representation: "... even as a black lesbian, I wouldn't want to be seen as this is how black lesbians are." DVD still.

vajo people to make subjective films about themselves and their culture, as a way both to supplement the work of outsider anthropologists and to explore broad questions about cross-cultural communication (Worth and Adair 1972). Nancy and Peter grew up on Navajo land, and Peter credits the experience with shaping the way he approached his own films: "Being in the minority, and sometimes the only white kid around, started me looking at everything from the eyes of an outsider. So in a sense, all my films, even if they are about my peers, are cultural studies" (in Dunlap 1996).

Before turning the camera on his own "tribe," Peter Adair made *Holy Ghost People* (1967), a vérité documentary about a Pentecostal community in rural West Virginia whose members speak in tongues and handle venomous snakes. The film's distanced and observational approach is worlds away from the intimate and voluble conversations that comprise *Word Is Out*. By structuring the later film as a collection of interviews, Adair sought to grant increased authority to the people onscreen, presenting them as subjects rather than objects and as the best experts on their own lives.

Subjects as primary witnesses

Film scholar Thomas Waugh recalls how gay filmmakers and cinephiles used the words "famine, drought, silence, and invisibility" to describe the state of gay audiovisual representation in the 1970s (1997, 107–08). Looking back on his 1980 proclamation that the famine was over, he speculates on what changed: "Suddenly at the turn of the decade, there did seem to be a few more documentary projects in sight, especially in the United States and Canada, films that would be able to get away with being underfunded, mediocre, local, or single-issue because they were no longer solitary voices in the wilderness" (ibid., 109). Although Waugh does not give full credit for the change to just one film, his account confirms that *Word Is Out* stood with only a few other gay and lesbian films at the late-1970s threshold between an earlier hunger for images and a newfound place at the media table. Gay and lesbian filmmakers working in the years after *Word Is Out* could now partially represent, selectively represent, and even misrepresent the range and complexity of gay and lesbian life without encountering the same scrutiny and outrage from a nascent, tenuously bound, and internally combustible movement. Nor would these later filmmakers feel the intense pressure that accompanies the thought that their film might be the only one about gay life seen by straight people and by closeted gay people, and thus taken as "gospel truth." The burden of representation had been lifted.

No "gospel truth"

C IS FOR COLLECTIVE

Peter Adair brought his sister Nancy into the project because he was committed to making a film that balanced men and women. At the same time, he did not feel that he could approach lesbians himself, and he did not know whom else to ask. "[T]he climate wasn't right. I didn't see how men could work with women, or how I'd even find a woman" (Peter Adair in N. Adair 1978, 273–74). Adair's statement indicates the extent to which lesbians and gay men were organizing and socializing separately before the late 1970s. He also believed that lesbian feminists would be reluctant to appear in a film produced exclusively by men, and that even if they did participate, they would not open up with a male interviewer as much as they would with a female interviewer. As Nancy Adair notes, she was "a handy lesbian to ask" (ibid., 267).

As the project grew in scope, the two siblings slowly brought other people onboard—some in a paid capacity and others initially as volunteers: Veronica Selver (a film editor and old friend of Peter's), Andrew Brown (hired as a camera assistant), Rob Epstein (brought in as a volunteer), and finally Lucy Massie Phenix (initially hired to help produce the film and manage the office). Neither Brown nor Epstein had significant experience in film production before *Word Is Out*. They came into the project by responding to an ad in a local magazine: "We are looking for a non-sexist person to work

40

on a documentary film on gay life. No experience necessary, just insane dedication and a cooperative spirit" (Epstein
1981, 9). Nancy Adair also learned the ins and outs of filmmaking by working on *Word Is Out*. By contrast, Selver and
Massie Phenix came to the project having already worked on
prestigious film projects: Selver as a sound editor for Milos
Forman's *One Flew Over the Cuckoo's Nest* (1975) and Massie
Phenix as an editor and one of the collective members behind the 1972 documentary *Winter Soldier*. Like Epstein,
both of them continue to make films today.[10]

Eventually all six filmmakers were involved in shooting
the interviews and making key decisions about the content
and shape of *Word Is Out*. Eventually, too, all were paid for
their work and had a stake in a percentage of the film: "We
were each paid one hundred dollars per week and owned a
portion of the film based on how much time we spent on
it" (N. Adair 1978, 307). Other paid staff members were
brought in during the postproduction stages of editing and
promotion. Only upon completion of *Word Is Out* did the six
main filmmakers call themselves the Mariposa Film Group,
taking the name from a street near Adair Films' San Francisco office. They knew that the word meant butterfly in
Spanish, but they were unaware that it was also often used

10. Neither Nancy Adair nor Andrew Brown pursued careers as
filmmakers. Today, Adair is a yoga teacher and an artist. Brown
earned a doctorate in psychology and runs a geriatric mental health
program in San Francisco.

as a derogatory term for homosexual (ibid., 295). Their use of the term "group" rather than "collective" suggests a hesitancy about the latter term's applicability, perhaps a feeling that they were always moving toward collectivity as an ideal rather than fully achieving it. During a press interview after the film's release, when somebody asked them when they had become a collective, the filmmakers replied, "In retrospect" (Epstein 1981, 10).

Epstein credits Nancy Adair for pushing the group to become a collective. Looking back, the change occurred in mid-1976, first at a series of meetings in the New York City apartment of a friend of the Adairs and then during a two-week retreat at Veronica Selver's mother's summer house in Cape Cod. The filmmakers, working individually or in groups of two, had completed the major round of video pre-interviews. As they shared their material with each other, they each felt some ownership over their tapes and over the people they had recruited as candidates for the film. Although Peter Adair was still the producer, he no longer felt that he alone was directing the film.[11] To facilitate discussion at the meetings and to help members reach consensus in their decisions, the group "passed the rattle," a technique Nancy Adair had acquired through her involvement with feminist collectives and which she attributed to a Native American ritual. The person hold-

---

11. For an in-depth account of Peter Adair's work as producer of *Word Is Out*, see P. Adair (1978).

FIGURE 3. Lucy Massie Phenix, Nancy Adair, and Andrew Brown settle into collectivity as they screen the video pre-interviews in Cape Cod. Photograph courtesy of the San Francisco Public Library, Mariposa Film Group, and Milliarium Films.

ing the "rattle" could talk as long as he or she wished (only when absolutely necessary were time limits introduced) and without interruption except when someone asked for clarification (N. Adair 1978, 275–76, 293–94; P. Adair n.d.; Epstein 1981, 10). By Nancy Adair's account, the group did not reach consensus easily. There were many different viewpoints among the members, as well as a tendency toward volatile expression, not least of all from the Adair siblings. Epstein makes the crucial point that he cannot imagine the process working if Peter Adair's basic design for the film had not already been in place and agreed upon (Epstein 1981, 9).

Film-maker conflict

D IS FOR DOCUMENTARY

The promotional website for the thirtieth-anniversary DVD of *Word Is Out* asserts that it was "the first feature-length documentary about lesbian and gay identity made by gay filmmakers" (*wordisoutmovie.com/project.htm*). This risks suggesting that no gay people had ever made a feature-length documentary about gay people before 1977. In fact, there were a few lengthy non-fiction films made before then by filmmakers such as Rosa von Praunheim and Andy Warhol. However, these films were experimental, theatrical, and campy, which is to say that they lacked the sobriety that is usually associated with the term "documentary."[12] Indeed, the performativity of the queer film canon has caused a good deal of trouble to projects of documentary classification. In 1994, Bill Nichols proposed a new subgenre of documentary, the "performative" mode, to account for films that are expressive, stylized, and theatrical; frequently more evocative than indexical; and, perhaps most troublingly, often

Performative as a film style [margin annotation]

---

12. In his 1992 book *Representing Reality*, Bill Nichols theorized documentary as a "discourse of sobriety," along with scientific, economic, and educational discourses. "Discourses of sobriety are sobering because they regard their relation to the real as direct, immediate, transparent" (3–4).

staged, acted, and pre-scripted.[13] Among his examples of this new mode, Nichols included the groundbreaking queer-of-color documentaries of the late 1980s and early 1990s, such as Isaac Julien's *Looking for Langston* (1989) and Marlon Riggs' *Tongues Untied* (1989). A few years later, Thomas Waugh took up Nichols' terminology and predated the rise of performative documentary to the gay and lesbian films of the 1970s, including in his list highly personal, playful, and formally experimental works by such filmmakers as Barbara Hammer, Tom Joslin, and Curt McDowell (1997). In the wake of these interventions, it is quite common for queer film scholars to mobilize the term "documentary" in a very fluid and capacious sense, approaching even the films of avant-garde pioneers like Jack Smith and Kenneth Anger as documentaries, which is to say as historical documents and photographic records of past queer life, and moreover as films that were invested in fabricating new queer realities, not new queer fictions, at the time they were made.[14]

Blur past reality + fiction

The definition of documentary has expanded to include

---

13. Here I am following Nichols and Waugh in using "performative" and "performativity" to refer mainly to the theatrical and performance-based qualities of these films. Without trying to confuse things, later in this book I will use "performativity" in the sense of the term developed in speech-act theory (see "W Is for Word").

14. See for instance Siegel (1997), as well as the larger collection in which his and Waugh's essays appear, Holmlund and Fuchs (1997).

FIGURE 4. Performative documentary: becoming Amazon in Barbara Hammer's *Superdyke* (1975). DVD still. Courtesy of Barbara Hammer.

so many experimental and "performative" films out of recognition that queer people frequently document themselves in non-sober, non-realistic ways. Interestingly, it is gay and lesbian "realist documentaries"—works in which gay and lesbian filmmakers harness the indexical properties of the camera in an apparently artifice-free way—that have a clearer date of origin and comprise a more easily bound canon. In a 1978 review of *Word Is Out* and Arthur Bressan's *Gay USA* (1978), Lee Atwell remarks with surprise that he can only think of one precedent of a gay filmmaker who took

a "direct-cinema" approach to gay subject matter: Kenneth
Robinson's *Some of Your Best Friends* (1971), a forty-minute
master's-thesis film from the University of Southern California. The film is a combination of interviews with gay and
lesbian activists in Los Angeles and New York—Don Kilhefner is featured most prominently—and footage of the 1970
Christopher Street West parade and a Gay Liberation Front
action against the 1970 Behavioral Modification Conference
at the Biltmore Hotel in Los Angeles. If one includes works
shorter than Robinson's film, it is clear that there were, in
fact, many direct-cinema documents of gay and lesbian life
prior to 1977. As Richard Dyer's extensive filmography of
works "from and for the movement" shows, most of the
1960s and 1970s gay celluloid record was comprised of short
works that took the form of either footage shot at a Pride
parade (or other public gay demonstration) or a brief filmed
interview with an openly gay or lesbian subject (1990, 231–
35). In this light, with its interviews and Pride parade mon-
tages, *Word Is Out* is a feature-length expansion of the many
short works that were already dotting the post-Stonewall
archive. And yet, in its quantitative increases over earlier
works—in length, funding, number of interviews assembled,
and number of viewers reached—*Word Is Out* marked a pro-
foundly qualitative shift in gay and lesbian representation.

The earlier observational and interview films tended to
be dashed off by amateurs and activists, or else they were
made by filmmakers like Pat Rocco and Christopher Larkin

[handwritten margin notes: Word Is Out, expand, short, non-performative, works]

who incorporated the footage into larger works that were more "performative" in structure.[15] What changed in the late 1970s was that the realist idiom became the framework for ambitious, expensive projects. In accounting for why six years had passed between Robinson's film and *Word Is Out*, Atwell cites the difficulties in securing funding for a non-sensational work on the subject of homosexuality, as well as the slow-to-open closet doors that prevented many gays and lesbians from being willing to appear on film. Although a number of the men and women in *Word Is Out* are activists in "everyday" drag, it is very clear when watching *Some of Your Best Friends* that *only* activists were willing to appear as openly gay on camera. Robinson drives this home in one sequence when he intercuts brightly lit scenes from activist-group meetings with a silhouetted interview of men and women involved in the Westside Discussion Group, a New York City organization that was dedicated to meeting the social and support needs of its members (e.g., organizing dancing lessons and bowling leagues) rather than to public education or political work. Atwell credits "the rising tide of anti-gay propaganda, spearheaded by Anita Bryant's Bible-thumping crusade," for creating a wider opening for gay realist documentary, both by provoking a new social con-

---

15. Larkin's 1974 film, *A Very Natural Thing*, is a fiction film about a gay male relationship, intercut with on-the-street interviews taken at the 1973 Gay Pride parade in New York.

FIGURE 5. What "ordinary" (that is to say, non-activist) gay people looked like onscreen before the late-1970s. DVD still from *Some of Your Best Friends* (1971). Courtesy of Kenneth Robinson.

sciousness among gays and lesbians and by helping to over-come earlier problems of funding and visibility (1978, 51).

Word Is Out shared the stage in the late 1970s with a number of other documentaries about gay and lesbian life that were more straightforwardly realist than performative: among them Bressan's *Gay USA*, Iris Films' *In the Best Interests of the Children* (1977), and Rosa von Praunheim's *Army of Lovers, or Revolt of the Perverts* (1979). Iris Films (Frances Reid, Elizabeth Stevens, and Cathy Zheutlin) premiered

FIGURE 6. Iris Films' *In the Best Interests of the Children* (1977). VHS screenshot. Courtesy of Women Make Movies.

their hour-long documentary about lesbian parenting and custody battles in the Bay Area a few months before *Word Is Out* had its December 1977 premiere (Iris Films 1978). What sets these late-1970s documentaries apart from what came before them is the collaboration in sober realism of the filmmakers and their subjects—the fact that neither the people behind nor in front of the camera camp it up. Warhol's films of the 1960s were arguably "sober" in their form—static camera, long takes, often no edits—but they placed their formal sobriety in a charged dialectic with the

Filmmaker + Subject = Realism

theatricality of the onscreen subject. Conversely, Hammer often filmed the everydayness of lesbian life, for instance in parts of *Women I Love* (1976), but she always transformed the material through formal experimentation. What distinguishes *Word Is Out* and the other realist documentaries of the late 1970s is the pact between filmmaker and subject that a sober presentation of gay life is both what is true and what is best.

E IS FOR EDITING

The final version of *Word Is Out* is only the tip of the iceberg. Just below the waterline is all the footage from the celluloid interviews that did not make the cut. Deeper down are more than 140 video pre-interviews, the vast majority with people who were not selected for the final film. These moving-image artifacts still exist. They are housed, along with many boxes of paper documentation, in the Peter Adair Papers at the San Francisco Public Library, and are available to anyone, like me, with the time and the initiative to look through them. The archive testifies to the filmmakers' prodigious labor and accomplishment in making *Word Is Out*. It also shows that they were committed to preserving more than just their final product. The materials in the archive enable endless speculation as to why certain people, and certain things that certain people said, did not make it into the film. Did the filmmakers feel that a particular speaker was too inarticulate? Not photogenic enough? Ideologically suspect? Too "negative" an image? Perhaps redundant with someone else whom they had already selected? Or was there simply not enough space to include them? In a few cases, the archive offers clues as to why decisions were made. But in most cases, it is silent.

Editing is the art of construction, deconstruction, and reconstruction. If, from one angle, making *Word Is Out* was about assembling sequences and building up a structure, from another angle it was about "carving away, carving away, and carving away" in order to discover the final film hidden within the mountain of raw footage (Mariposa Film Group 1978, 11). The history of the film is in many ways a history of edits. Fundraising did not take off until Peter Adair created a composite of clips from the first video pre-interviews that emulated the intended structure of the final film (N. Adair 1978, 272–73). The archive contains a videotape labeled "Master Fall 1974" that presents intercut interviews with about twenty subjects, of whom only Whitey Fladden is included in the final film.[16] Her testimony functions as the tape's structuring thread. The video edit is very rough, with a good deal of visual distortion and with sound and picture in sync but not always cutting out at the same time: the sound of a person speaking often bleeds over into the next image. Another tape, not dated but labeled "Who Are We?" (the project's early working title), features Fladden and four others from the final film, indicating that it was made a little later when the film's cast was beginning to coalesce. This

---

16. In Nancy Adair's account of the film's making, she says she conducted six video interviews, including the one with Fladden, in the spring of 1975, which suggests either that the tape is mislabeled or that her memory is off a little bit (1978, 271). Either way, the tape is clearly from very early in the film's history, and it fits Adair's description of the first video composite (ibid., 274).

tape also includes about twenty other people, many of them not on the earlier tape.

Together the two tapes give a sense of some of the alternate paths the project might have taken. For example, the second tape presents a lesbian couple with children, but they are very different from Pam Jackson and Rusty Millington, the working-class, butch/femme couple of the final film. The women on the tape are more androgynous in their gender presentations, apparently middle-class, and they speak academic/activist feminism fluently. *Word Is Out* would have been a different film had this couple been used instead. A third version of the film might have included both couples. Such speculation likely seems pointless, but upon encountering the archive it is also inevitable. The video pre-interviews and the celluloid outtakes comprise a database of (potentially) non-hierarchized material about gay and lesbian life in the mid- to late-1970s, from which one can imagine cutting together a number of other composite videos and films with different emphases, even different politics, than the version of *Word Is Out* that we have.

By March 1976, the Mariposa Film Group had filmed eight people—Pat Bond, Whitey Fladden, Elsa Gidlow, Pam Jackson, Tede Mathews, George Mendenhall, Rusty Millington, and Rick Stokes—and from this footage they created the first film composite. Through community screenings of this early cut (which was roughly three hours in length), the filmmakers got a sense of specific gaps in representation that

Handwritten margin note: Avoided other issues- gender, feminism?

they and the audience members felt needed to be filled in, ~~Diversity~~
including the absence of people of color and people from
outside the San Francisco Bay Area. In late spring and early
summer of 1976 they broke off for a marathon round of
video interviews across the US, and then, in a whirlwind six
weeks later that year, they conducted the last major round of
film interviews with people selected from the tapes. Most of
1977 was devoted to sound and picture editing of the final
film, but editing can hardly be said to have begun when the
filming stopped: the filmmakers had been busy assembling,
disassembling, and reassembling their material the entire
time.

For Peter Adair, editing was one of the biggest challenges
in making *Word Is Out*, but it was also the film's greatest artistic legacy. Looking back on the film in the early 1990s, he
said that its aesthetic form "was radical for [its] time and has
since been copied ad infinitum by other films ... This tech- *Unique*
nique is used a lot now, the simultaneous telling of multiple *storytelling*
stories but I think we originated it" (P. Adair 1993). He was
saddened that *Word Is Out*, while often appreciated as social
activism and as a historical document, has seldom been recognized as a work of art or cinematic innovation.[17]

---

17. Adair also reflects on the artistic accomplishment of *Word Is Out*
in a video interview included as a special feature on the DVD of his
1991 film *Absolutely Positive*.

F IS FOR FEMINISM

As *Word Is Out* neared completion, Peter Adair and Rob Epstein expressed concern that despite the collective's commitment to gender parity the film was out of balance: the women were overshadowing the men. As Epstein explained:

> The male consciousness was never as clear or directed as the female consciousness. There was a feminist personality and analysis for the group to assume—one that included all women—but there was no larger male personality that included all gay men in the same way. It would be oversimplification to say this was merely a reflection of the men working in the film, or the men working on the film. It is rather a reflection of most gay men and the gay men's movement which limits itself, for the most part, to dealing with "rights" without a broader overview. (Nancy Adair 1978, 304)

[handwritten margin note: Larger female vs. male personality]

Although it is not fully clear what Epstein means by "larger male personality," he seems to yearn for a shared identity and bond among gay men that would match the sisterhood fostered by the institutions and practices of cultural feminism.[18] There are indications that other viewers of the film

[handwritten margin note: Unifying cultural feminism]

18. "Cultural feminism" is often defined on the one hand as the

felt similarly. As Nancy Adair noted soon after the film's release, "Often people (usually men) have told us that the film
is more heavily weighted toward women" (ibid., 304). By
contrast, in his early review of the film, Lee Atwell found
that "while the film's most cogent intellectual arguments
come from women, its strongest emotional arguments
emerge from men" (1978, 53–54).

Intellectual + emotional arguments

Word Is Out is a far cry from the ecstatic, erotic visions
of Barbara Hammer's films and the work of other artists associated with 1970s cultural feminism. Yet clearly the film
is drawn to the aesthetics and energy of this movement: to
women's rural gatherings and experiments in communal living as felt in the scenes with Whitey Fladden, Elsa Gidlow,
and Ann Samsell, as well as to women's music in the form
of the prominently featured songs of Trish Nugent. Most
of the other filmmakers credit Nancy Adair for the film's
strong feminist content. In her 1978 account of working on
the film, Adair writes that she came into the project as a
"bar dyke," uninvolved in explicit feminist activism (285).
Indeed, during a public screening of an early print of the
film, held in March 1976 in San Francisco, she was horrified

---

network of feminist cultural forms (e.g., music, films, journals,
ritual celebrations) that developed in the 1970s, including the small
business structures forged to sustain them, and on the other hand
as the mode of feminist activism and theory that embraced and
explored essentialism and separatism. These two aspects of 1970s
feminist experience often overlapped, but not always.

to see "some of the staunchest lesbian feminists [she] knew walk in." She had been careful not to invite them (it was Selver who had done so). After the screening, which according to Adair brought not only gay men and lesbians but also "gays from various political factions" into conversation, she "was beaming and feeling very different about the feminists" (ibid., 286–287).[19]

Adair was eager to find a rural women's community to include in the film. With Massie Phenix and her brother, she filmed a conversation among twelve members of the North Carolina group Triangle Area Lesbian Feminists (TALF). It proved difficult to integrate a group protagonist into a project focused on individuals, so the filmmakers pulled Linda Marco and Ann Samsell out for individual portraits. Adair felt that Samsell represented her own values more than anyone else in the film: "She is … a role model for me; she represents a spirit of the new lesbian that I so strongly respond to and identify with" (ibid., 301). Adair does not explain what she means by "new lesbian" or make it clear

"New lesbian"

19. Although in her account of the film's making, Nancy Adair presents herself as politically naïve and uninitiated before she began working on the project, she had been involved in student protests at San Francisco State University in the late 1960s and had co-founded the Southwestern Female Rights Union with Helaine Harris in the early 1970s (Echols 1989, 224). Among the video pre-interviews, there is one in which Trish Nugent interviews Adair. In the video, Adair mentions that she traveled to Cuba as part of the Venceremos Brigade.

FIGURE 7. The representative "new lesbian": Ann Samsell in *Word Is Out*. DVD still.

why Samsell fits the bill. Among Samsell's attributes, she was a practicing veterinarian and thus a "professional" (one of the few who was willing to appear on film [N. Adair and C. Adair 1978, 183]), she valued and was close to her family, she experimented with alternative lesbian cultural and community forms (she lived on a farm in a relationship with two other women), and she expressed a feminist consciousness without being overtly politicized: "I considered myself, and was considered when I was in veterinary school, a feminist, even though I was not out marching or anything." In her

Careers at stake

account of the film's making, Adair recalls, "I was looking for a woman who could represent the *spirit* of lesbian-feminism rather than the rhetoric. I wanted someone who could translate, through the lens of her life story, the feelings I had had at women's events in California" (1978, 291).

Word Is Out integrates men and women at the level of editing but not mise-en-scène, which is to say that gay men and lesbians virtually never occupy the frame at the same time. In this way, despite cultural feminism's insistence on female-specific understandings of homosexuality, the film is able to fold it into a gender-integrated presentation of gay life. As Selver noted in a 1978 interview, women and men are only superficially brought together in the film; neither the film nor the interview subjects ever deal with the "differences" between them, by which she presumably means sexual cultures and degrees of feminist consciousness. However, she goes on to say that the film encourages viewers to pick up where it leaves off and to make connections across the gender divide (Russo 1978, 31).

Invites commentary on gender divide

Some of the film's avowed feminists seem to have been more easily integrated into the project than others. Elsa Gidlow stands out as a particularly resistant subject who, nevertheless, happily was included. The seventy-seven-year-old poet is remarkably straightforward but also less compliant with the interviewers than the younger feminists like Ann Samsell, Cynthia Gair, Linda Marco, and Betty Powell. Nancy Adair first met Gidlow at a Country Women's

Older vs. younger lesbians

Figure 8. A different type of "conversation": Elsa Gidlow enjoys lunch with a group of younger lesbians. DVD still.

Festival in Northern California, and she was immediately struck by the older woman's beauty, vigor, and stately presence. Born in England in 1898, Gidlow grew up in Quebec, moved to New York in her early twenties, and then to San Francisco a decade later at the dawn of the Great Depression. Although she was a participant in the spaces of cultural feminism during the 1970s, she expressed bemusement at younger women's politicization of their lesbian identities and the importance they placed on coming-out narratives (N. Adair 1978, 281–82). There is a moment in *Word Is Out*

political identity

when Gidlow warmly greets a group of younger women in front of her Marin County home. When everyone is inside and seated around the kitchen table, Adair asks her to discuss her reservations about being in the film. The older woman explains, openly and without anger, "I understand your point of view in this: you have a structure and you want to fit your characters into it. But this happens to be a character who doesn't want to be pushed around or put into a context that she doesn't feel is true to her." Over a simple meal of wine, fruit, and cheese, the women proceed to have a lively conversation about the pros and cons of lesbian militancy and the value of political calls to come out. It is the only moment of "conversation" in the film that is not restricted to the dyad of filmmaker and subject.[20]

[handwritten margin note: Character molds]

[handwritten margin note: Differences w/in the group of lesbians]

---

20. As further evidence of Gidlow's unruliness, it was on her insistence that Peter Adair agreed to compensate all of the interview participants with a percentage of the film's profits (N. Adair 1978, 282). For more on Gidlow, see her autobiography *ELSA: I Come With My Songs*, which was published in 1986, the year of her death. For more on her formative years in Canada, see Higgins (2006).

G IS FOR GEARHART

Despite wanting Ann Samsell in the film because she represented the spirit rather than the rhetoric of lesbian feminism, Nancy Adair eventually decided that *Word Is Out* also needed Sally Gearhart as "an articulate spokesperson representing the lesbian-feminist view" (1978, 304). Gearhart was forty-five years old at the time of her interview. Born and raised in Virginia, for many years she taught speech and drama at various Christian colleges and state universities in Texas and the Midwest and was a vocal supporter of conservative political causes and cultural norms. The movements of the 1960s changed her life. She arrived in California in 1970 at the height of women's and gay liberation. Hired in 1973 as a professor of speech and communications at San Francisco State University, she helped to form one of the nation's first radical women's studies programs and became the first open lesbian to receive tenure at an American university. Gearhart is a useful figure through which to explore the relationship between lesbian separatism and integrated gay and lesbian rights organizing. The year *Word Is Out* appeared in theaters and on television, she was gaining fame simultaneously as a gay liberal activist and a theorist of lesbian separatism.

In 1978, Gearhart campaigned with Harvey Milk against the Briggs Initiative. Together they chaired A United Fund:

[handwritten margin note: Sally Gearhart — lesbian separatism?]

Figure 9. Sally Gearhart and Harvey Milk appear in drag as "Mama and Papa USA" for a debate with California State Senator John Briggs on the KQED series *A Closer Look*. DVD still from *The Times of Harvey Milk* (1984). Courtesy of Rob Epstein.

To Defeat the Briggs Initiative, an organization designed to raise and distribute money to groups throughout California engaged in "No on 6" organizing. They also teamed up to debate State Senator John Briggs at a series of community forums. One of these debates occurred on *A Closer Look*, a news program produced by the Bay Area PBS affiliate KQED and broadcast throughout the state in the autumn of 1978, only a few weeks before the national broadcast of *Word Is Out*. It is in her capacity as liberal rights organizer and friend of Milk that Gearhart appears in Rob Epstein's 1984 documentary *The Times of Harvey Milk*. In the film, she remembers having strategized with Milk about how they should appear on television and agreeing that they should present an image of "Mama and Papa USA, as neat and conservative as we possibly could." They appeared in smart suits and proceeded to rake Briggs over the coals for his unsubstantiated claim that homosexuals pose a greater threat of child molestation than heterosexuals.

presentation of respectability on tv

In 1978 Gearhart also published her science-fiction novel, *The Wanderground: Stories of the Hill Women*, which is now considered a classic of lesbian-separatist writing. A work of speculative fiction set in a world parallel to our own, *The Wanderground* assembles a series of interrelated tales about a group of women who have fled the male-dominated city to live together in the countryside. There, in isolation from men, they develop powers of telekinesis, flight, and telepathic communication, this last not only with each other but also with the animals, plants, and inorganic objects of their environment. A significant portion of the book is devoted to women's interpersonal relationships as they engage in the ongoing work of living together; for instance, how they deal with shared work, fading love affairs, personality clashes, and eruptions of non-feminist behavior. The book is at once a utopian and a practical exploration of separatist community formation. The gay-rights struggles of 1977 and 1978 brought many cultural feminists into liberal politics. This

FIGURE 10. Sally Gearhart is confronted with the big question: "Are you a lesbian separatist?" DVD still.

development came as no surprise to self-defined "radical feminists," who already considered cultural and liberal feminism to be two sides of the same coin (Redstockings 1975; Echols 1989, 243–86). Nevertheless, for committed lesbian separatists the transition necessitated a negotiation of widely disparate political philosophies and social visions. The paradox of Gearhart's commitments is felt in Part Three of *Word Is Out*. Throughout the film, she is warm and charismatic, decked out in shades of lavender and pastel blue and seated cross-legged with a banjo hanging on the wall behind her.

But when Lucy Massie Phenix asks her, "Are you a lesbian separatist?" Gearhart is pinned to the wall in close-up as she searches for a response. This was precisely the question she had been brought into the film to answer.

Gearhart provides a lengthy response. She stresses the importance of the separatist project, but also its impossibility. "How can we separate from the system?" At the same time, she points to the historical fact of separatism in a broader sense: "Women are leaving men by the droves in this country, in greater numbers than statistics probably show." Elsewhere in the interview, beyond what is shown in the film, she clarifies her position further: "I'm not saying that every woman has got to separate from every man. But I think there has to be a large enough separation of women from men to make a qualitative difference in history" (N. Adair and C. Adair 1978, 258).

Fear of women not needing men?

Today Gearhart has tempered her relationship with separatism. During my own interview with her, she recalled with humor that Alice Echols, a strong critic of cultural feminism, once took her to task for having stated that the pursuit of orgasm was an inherently masculinist, goal-oriented approach to sexual intimacy and that it had no place in a feminist erotics.[21] Also with humor, she referred to some

21. I interviewed Gearhart on March 25, 2009. She still writes lesbian utopian science fiction and she considers herself to be "a recovering political activist, who's backsliding." It is worth mentioning that at the height of the sex wars in the 1980s, Gearhart

of the separatist positions she and others held in the 1970s as "fascist," but she made it clear too that she continues to value and defend the separatist project. "I'll fight for separatist rights until the day I die. Because I do believe that for most women it is a process. And for some women, it's not a process; it really is an identity." When I asked Gearhart how she had reconciled her commitment to separatism with her decision to participate in *Word Is Out*, she grew thoughtful. She saw the validity of my question, and she was certain that she had struggled with this issue at the time. But she also felt certain that she had never hesitated to participate in the film. She shared Nancy Adair's commitment to making sure the film contained a strong representation of lesbian feminism.[22]

As Gearhart discussed the connections between the separatist and integrationist currents of her life and activism in the 1970s, she relayed stories about the writing of her books. She remembered that when she wrote the majority of *The Wanderground* she felt like she was channeling the material. By contrast, when she wrote the final chapters she felt like she was struggling consciously to bring her thoughts togeth-

---

discovered a penchant for S/M and renounced many of her earlier, essentialist attitudes about sex and sexuality.

22. Gearhart's recollection is supported by the sentiments expressed in a note she wrote to Nancy and Casey Adair as they were preparing the accompanying book to the film (Peter Adair Papers, box 44, folder 18).

er. Presumably written around 1977, these chapters explore what happens when the Hill Women decide to meet with the Gentles: men who have renounced patriarchal ways, including sex with women, and who manifest a feminist consciousness. In the third-to-last chapter, a few women from the Wanderground meet with four Gentles, and the two sides begin to work through their mutual distrust and animosity. The women discover that the Gentles have begun to develop telekinetic powers of their own, which the women had thought impossible for men. By presenting an image of a feminist gay male commune, one that reflects a lesbian-separatist ethos yet respects the autonomy of women-only spaces, *The Wanderground* qualifiedly suggests the possibility of non-exploitative, cross-gender coalition. Perhaps *Word Is Out*, with its tentative steps toward the coexistence of sensitive men and strong women, is not so much at odds with the book's final vision.

M/F
collaboration

Word Is Out features Harry Hay, who is considered by many to be the forefather of contemporary gay activism because of his role in founding the Mattachine Society, a pioneering US gay activist organization, in the early 1950s (D'Emilio 1983, 57–74). Hay is interviewed along with his companion, John Burnside. They repose together on a blanket at the base of a large tree, in front of their home near San Juan Pueblo in the Rio Grande River Valley of northern New Mexico. The two men had moved there from Los Angeles at the beginning of the decade in part so that Hay could immerse himself in his ongoing investigations of homosexuality and transgenderism within Pueblo Indian history and culture. In 1979, not long after the release of *Word Is Out*, Hay and Burnside returned to Los Angeles where they founded the Radical Faeries with Don Kilhefner and Mitch Walker.

Throughout his life, Hay sought to uncover the essence of gay male experience. His theory of male homosexuality was in many ways a continuation of Edward Carpenter's model from the beginning of the twentieth century, which was inspired in turn by the poetry of Walt Whitman. Carpenter saw homosexuals as a special "third sex," combining elements of the other two, and therefore inherently more sensitive, artistic, and gifted, and with a valuable role to play in society. Like Carpenter, Hay's research into "primitive"

FIGURE 11. John Burnside and Harry Hay lounging in front of their home in New Mexico. DVD still.

cultures was an effort to establish and get in touch with the transhistorical, essential truth of this claim, as were the back-to-the-land practices of the Radical Faeries and other gay rural collectives. Hay's theory of gay male essence also mirrored the magical and primitivist understandings of lesbianism circulating in cultural-feminist spaces. (The Faeries are a bit like the Gentles that Gearhart describes in *The Wanderground*.) In other ways too, Hay's thought seems to rework lesbian-feminist ideas for gay men, as in his assertion that male homosexual relationships were fundamentally different from heterosexual ones because they were subject-subject

Radical Faeries — in touch w/ nature

Hay: Homosexual: subject-subject
Heterosexual: subject-object

relations rather than subject-object ones based on inequality and domination (Hay 1976).

Word Is Out presents Hay as an affable older gentleman who is in sync with the film's larger, liberal understanding of gay life. The film does not explore how Hay's belief system and approach to gay liberation might run contrary to its own. For instance, although Hay and Burnside were companions for forty years, Hay was not an exponent of monogamy (Bronski 2002). And although he supported the cause of gay rights, he was vocally against assimilation (Levy 2000). He was also opposed to the purging of undesirables so that only a respectable subset of gays and lesbians could achieve rights, as evinced by the infamous "Harry Hay incident" when he marched alone in the 1986 Gay Pride parade in Los Angeles wearing a sandwich board that read "NAMBLA Walks With Me," a gesture in support of the North American Man-Boy Love Association, which had been banned from participating in the parade (Timmons 1990, 295–96).

Hay often complained that he was treated as "the Dinosaur Duchess" of gay activism, dragged out as a pioneer and a relic of the gay past, but without anybody expressing interest in his political analysis of current issues (Timmons 1990, 294; Bronski 2002). *Word Is Out* never mentions Hay's Communist organizing, and more surprisingly, it never mentions his role in founding the Mattachine Society. As Michael Bronski pointed out in a corrective obituary for Hay (corrective of the sanitizing of Hay's image and politics in the

[handwritten margin note: Harry Hay's past filtered]

first round of mainstream obituaries), the film "portrayed Hay and Burnside as paragons of gay domesticity" (2002). At the same time, Stuart Timmons' biography of Hay (written in close consultation with Hay and published while he was still alive) suggests that the film helped put Hay back on the map, and that Hay was pleased to hear that the moment when he takes Burnside's hand after berry-picking touched so many people in the audience (1990, 247; see also Guthman 1981, 37).

During the film shoot, Peter Adair did ask Hay about Mattachine. He also inquired how Burnside and Hay's approach to gay liberation differed from the dominant gay liberal approach:

> ADAIR: There's a sort of force in a lot of the gay movement to say that gay people are like everyone else, that we are different only in that we have different choices about with whom we want to go to bed …

> HAY: At this point, I'll stick my neck way out and say that in my estimation what you have described is what I call homosexual. Those people who are exactly like heteros except that they have a slight difference in their sexual and affectional preferences. But gay people are people who, maybe from birth, have known that they have a multidimensional quality which separates them from other people. And in this

[Handwritten margin note: Harry Hay: same in bed, different everywhere else]

respect, you might say that gay people are almost opposite from everybody else, except in bed. Because after all, since the sexual revolution, everybody does everything to everybody. We are different from everybody else, except in bed, I think. (N. Adair and C. Adair 1978, 244–46)

There is a world of difference between gay liberal essentialism, which boils down to a born-this-way variation in sexual object-choice as the only and negligible thing that distinguishes a gay individual from a straight one, and Hay's expansive vision of a "multidimensional" essence that infuses every aspect of a gay person's existence and refuses to be contained in the privatized space of the bedroom. Although the filmmakers included an exploration of Gearhart's views on separatism and essentialism in the final film, the shape of Hay's thinking, not to mention Burnside's, is hardly even glimpsed.

I IS FOR INTERVIEW

In planning *Word Is Out*, Peter Adair was inspired by Marcel Ophüls' *Le chagrin et la pitié* (*The Sorrow and the Pity*), a 1969 documentary about the French Resistance and Collaboration during World War II. For Adair, the truth-value and political impact of Ophüls' film were in direct correlation with its lack of style and polish. "That film had so much meaning for me. And that film was doing everything 'wrong.' It was in black-and-white. It was four and a half hours long. It was full of jump cuts. It had the worst photography. And it was talking heads. But I could have sat there another three hours watching it!" (N. Adair 1978, 217).[23]

Despite his stated appreciation of bad photography and mediocre form, Adair thought through the cinematography and visual form of *Word Is Out* very carefully. He devised a number of methods for shooting the interviews, all of them *Intimacy* designed to increase the viewer's sense of intimacy with the onscreen subjects (Mariposa Film Group 1978, 11). The number of people present at each shoot was kept to a minimum, so that the interview subjects would not feel overwhelmed. In fact, in a particularly innovative move, it was a

23. Adair was also inspired by Studs Terkel's 1974 book *Working*, a thematically arranged collection of oral histories of people from various walks of life talking about their jobs.

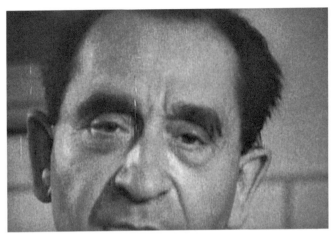

FIGURE 12. Marcel Ophüls' *The Sorrow and the Pity* (1969): a captivating documentary that does everything "wrong" when it comes to film form. DVD still. Courtesy of Milestone Films.

[handwritten margin note: Cameraman as interviewer]

rule that the camera operator also be the interviewer, so that the subjects would not find it artificial to look directly at the lens when answering questions. This technique also fostered an organic connection between the flow of the interview and its visual form, because the same person was orchestrating both. For instance, the camera operator could zoom in or out in connection with the questions she asked and the answers she received (see "Z Is for Zoom").

There were non-fiction films featuring interviews with gay subjects before *Word Is Out*, but they tended to be much less "conversational." The early films do not exhibit the same formal and ethical concerns with constructing a scene of egalitarian exchange between interviewer and interviewee. In Andy Warhol's *Screen Test #2* (1965) and Shirley Clarke's *Portrait of Jason* (1967), the interviewers cruelly probe their subjects—Mario Montez and Jason Holliday—seeking to catch them up in lies and contradictions. *Screen Test #2* features an offscreen interviewer, Ronald Tavel, interviewing Montez in drag, directing her to perform embarrassing acts, and finally provoking her to disrobe and admit she's a man. *Portrait of Jason* presents a marathon interview with a black gay hustler who is at first encouraged to tell amusing, theatrical stories about himself, and then driven to tears through drink, exhaustion, and heckling. These films try to get at "the truth" of their subjects by provoking a breakdown of their performed selves and the revelation of something vulnerable and presumably more real (i.e., not performed) lying beneath. At the same time, the films suggest that the truth of queer subjects exists, paradoxically, not behind or beyond the performance, but in the dialectical relationship between the performed persona and the person who performs it. In both films, the interview subjects resist and elude the various understandings of who they are.[24]

Word Is Out largely eschews such a sadistic and manipula-

---

24. For discussions of the sadistic design of *Screen Test #2* and *Portrait of Jason*, and of their particular constructions of the "truth" of queer subjects, see Crimp (2002) and Butts (2007).

FIGURE 13. Breaking through the performance to the "real" person underneath, late-1960s style: Jason Holliday at the end of *Portrait of Jason* (1967). DVD still. Courtesy of Milestone Films and Wendy Clarke.

tive approach to its interviews. This makes it all the more striking when, during a few key moments, the filmmakers take up a more interrogational style. Nancy Adair discusses one of these moments in her account of the film shoot with Pat Bond, the ex-Women's Army Corps nurse who speaks at length in the first part of the film about lesbian subcultures during World War II and in postwar San Francisco. Adair knew that Bond was a great storyteller from time spent with her at Maud's, a lesbian bar in the city. As many reviewers

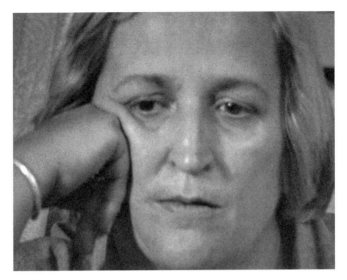

FIGURE 14. Breaking through the performance to the "real" person underneath, late-1970s style: Pat Bond falls silent in *Word Is Out*. DVD still.

of the film noted, Bond is a wonderfully engaging *raconteuse*: regaling us with stories as she smokes cigarette after ciga-
rette in front of her typewriter, and getting up as needed to lampoon gendered ways of walking. Bond was able to launch a career from her performance in *Word Is Out*: a few weeks after the film's premiere she began a nightclub act in San Francisco, and soon afterward began touring the country with two one-woman shows, *Conversations with Pat Bond* and *Gerty Gerty Stein is Back Back Back* (Guthman 1981, 37).

Pat Bond and her comedic performance

It is clear from Adair's account that she understood Bond to be a person who hid her true self behind a comic façade. For the film shoot, she wanted to capture Bond's stories and the truth behind them, in that order. She brought her brother into the interview to begin the questions, so that Bond could tell her jokes to a fresh audience. After this, the thrust of the interview changed:

> When I took over the interview, Pat was already tired and hot from the lights. It was getting dark, so that the window next to her eventually became pitch black—another uncontrollable variable that adds to the emotional impact of the film. I used about two mags and felt I was getting nowhere with her.
>
> I decided to be more responsive and more challenging, feeling that we had nothing to lose. Pat had answered negatively when I asked a question about lesbian support, so I asked a question which developed from her negative response: if she had had no support, how could she stand it? It elicited an emotional response, a frustrated response, and a long silence following it. In those few seconds she expresses for all of us our sense of powerlessness, our resignation, and our alienation. Pat stopped telling her jokes and showed a part of herself that was protected by them. (1978, 283)

strategize for truth

Adair's account mirrors the making and narrative arc of *Portrait of Jason* (Clarke's shoot with Jason Holliday lasted more than eight hours), at the same time that her avowed identification and sympathy for Bond sets the films apart. It is true that Bond's silence is an especially magnetic moment in *Word Is Out.* Yet it is also clear that the interview technique serves to discipline her as a subject. Bond occupies the space of "The Early Years," which is to say the space of the pre-Stonewall closet, the duality of the passing experience, and pre-feminist butch/femme "role-playing." Although Nancy Adair identifies and sympathizes with Bond's use of humor as a defensive shield, she sees the moment when Bond breaks out of performance and reflects inwardly as a step forward—a move toward self-awareness. Confrontational interview techniques are infrequent in the film, but when they do appear they are reserved for members of the older generation, such as Sally Gearhart, Elsa Gidlow, and George Mendenhall. These techniques are apparently unnecessary for the younger interviewees who make their appearance in Part Two, "Growing Up." This generation seems to arrive before the camera already interpellated as authentic gay subjects: they are thoughtful, calm, undivided in self-presentation, and they never act out.

[Margin annotations: "Older vs. younger subjects" and "Younger → more authentic w/out prompting"]

K IS FOR KQED

Before 1973, when he began working on his proposal for what would become *Word Is Out*, Peter Adair worked for two years in the National Programming Division of KQED television, the Bay Area PBS affiliate (P. Adair 1974).[25] He would maintain a close relationship with KQED throughout his career, including with the production and exhibition of his two major works about HIV/AIDS, *The AIDS Show* (1986) and *Absolutely Positive* (1991) (see "R Is for Retroviral"). But before public television began to accommodate films with gay content—a change that *Word Is Out* helped to bring about—Adair was frustrated in his role as an in-house producer. According to his sister, "he decided he could not make another film until he made one about himself—for and about homosexuals" (N. Adair 1978, 269). Striking out on his own, he eventually landed a $50,000 start-up grant for his project; oddly enough, it came not from KQED but from WNET, the New York City PBS affiliate. The project very quickly blew up beyond what this grant would cover, and the filmmakers found it necessary to raise the majority of their funding from individual investors.

Project outgrew grant from WNET

---

25. Before this, in addition to his own film, *Holy Ghost People* (1967), he served as a camera operator for Albert and David Maysles' direct-cinema classic *Gimme Shelter* (1970), about the Rolling Stones and their notorious 1969 Altamont concert.

Considering the extent of the project's independence, it is a bit unfair that Thomas Waugh, in an essay written after attending a 1976 community feedback/fundraising screening in New York, criticized it as a work of "establishment TV." In doing so, Waugh was noting the link to WNET and the advance agreement that the film would screen on PBS; however, he was also responding to the film's carefully non-controversial presentation of its potentially volatile subject matter. Having listened to the filmmakers' framing of the project at the screening, he notes: "One strategy of the collective that seems fairly definite and that many radical gays have found dismaying is the soft-pedaling of explicit political rhetoric and analysis in the interviews—in short, according to some critics, censorship." According to Waugh, "Adair believes that such rhetoric will alienate nonpoliticized gays and prevent them from coming out and that films like *Hearts and Minds* [Peter Davis, 1974], with its explicit political viewpoint, talk down to their audiences from a position of righteousness" (1977, 27). Adair responded angrily to Waugh's analysis in an interview with Vito Russo conducted after a New York screening of the final film. He talks of being "trashed … in a socialist film newspaper called *Jump Cut*. They had seen a rough cut a long time ago and said that certain concessions were made to get the film on PBS television, which is crap. This film is what we made it. We're aware of what we want to talk to our audience about." Adair insists that he and the other filmmakers in no way "buckled

Accused of censorship + selling out

under for commercial purposes." When Russo asks where the *Jump Cut* writer got the idea, Adair responds tersely: "Made it up" (Russo 1978, 43).[26]

There is a thick file of correspondence between Adair and WNET housed in the Peter Adair Collection at the San Francisco Public Library (box 33, folder 7). Much of it concerns Adair's efforts to materialize the funding that the station pledged. Although some of the letters pertain to both parties' early efforts to secure the right of final cut, I found no indication in the file or anywhere else that the station ever asked for changes to be made to the film or that conflicts arose over its content. Adair's vision of a non-controversial film that would convey its message without political rhetoric seems to have met the standards of public television without need for further negotiation. (The fact that the film enjoyed critical success in its theatrical run, months before its television airdate, may also have allayed any concerns the station may have had.) If *Word Is Out* is an embedded work of "establishment TV," it was more likely through Adair's formation at KQED than through his specific negotiations with WNET. He had already learned the rules of the game

---

26. A decade later, Waugh provided a lengthier and more complex analysis of how gay and lesbian filmmakers negotiate mainstream media channels and various kinds of censorship in their efforts to bring gay-positive content to mass audiences (Waugh 1988). In this essay, as in all his subsequent writings, he is much less harsh with *Word Is Out*.

when it came to making films for public television, and he had already worked out his strategies for getting gay content onto the screen.

In the wrap-up of his discussion of the rough-cut screening, Waugh predicts that any "radical" effects of the film will arise not from the views articulated by its onscreen subjects, but from "the film's documentary ontology itself."

> I mean this in the same way that the early feminist films, modest records of ordinary women talking about their lives, proved invaluable as a consciousness-raising tool in the women's movement, regardless of the level of awareness reached by the subjects on the screen. If the lively debate triggered by the trial version is matched on a larger scale when *Who Are We?* is finally broadcast, the collective and the radical gay community will have no cause to complain. (Waugh 1977, 28)

Effect of whole film vs. individual subjects

In the context of television home-viewing, it is unlikely that the film provoked the same "lively debate" between liberals and radicals that energized the community pre-screenings. Nevertheless, Waugh proved prescient in linking the "documentary ontology" of the film to its national PBS broadcast. Through television the film reached a viewership likely in the low millions, an exponential leap over the many thousands who saw it in theaters. Perhaps more importantly, on television it entered the homes of closeted and isolated les-

TV → wider audience -like the web (YouTube)

bians and gay men, and it also reached a number of intolerant straight people who would never have paid the price of a ticket.

The filmmakers included a mailing address at the end of the film, inviting viewers' reactions and general inquiries. They received more than a thousand letters, the majority from people who saw the film on PBS.[27] The letters are not without complaint. One woman expresses disappointment over the lack of representation of bisexuality in the film. Another writer is viciously unhappy about the film's overrepresentation of "long-haired hippie sissies." Perhaps my favorite letter criticizes the film, of all things, for showing too many people playing with their feet! The critiques, though, are few and far between. The majority of the letters express praise and gratitude for the film. A fourteen-year-old viewer writes that he was born homosexual but that he was never able to associate his experience with anyone else's until seeing the film, and that for the first time he feels good about

[handwritten margin note: Critiques on diversity + representation]

---

27. The original letters are not in the Adair Collection. However, there is a document in which Peter Adair describes the fan mail and presents a selection of letters, six in their entirety and excerpts from twenty-eight others (box 55, folder 14). My examples are taken from Adair's selection. The website promoting the thirtieth-anniversary DVD of *Word Is Out* includes a "Share Your Story" feature. Many of the contributors tell similar stories about the impact of seeing the film on PBS in 1978 (*wordisoutmovie.blogspot.com*). A few of the accounts mention local PBS affiliates that, without explanation, failed to air the program when it was scheduled to appear.

himself. Other writers say that they do not know yet if they are gay, straight, or bisexual, but express how wonderful it is to see a gay person with whom they can relate. A woman writes that she was so energized after seeing the film on TV that she went out that night and danced, something she had not been able to do in a long time. Through its national PBS broadcast, *Word Is Out* seems to have achieved the goals and had the impact that Adair intended for the project from the beginning. The film's "documentary ontology"—the simple power of witnessing actual people who are open and accepting of their own homosexuality—positively affected the lives of many viewers.

Stifling heteronormative culture

L IS FOR LIBERAL

> There were certain premises that were very fundamental.
> The film would deal with both women and men, it would
> be portraits of people intercut with each other, and it
> would never take an overt, political, rhetorical stance.
> —Peter Adair, in a 1978 interview with Vito Russo

To use the term casually, many things are "liberal" about
Word Is Out, for instance its earnest presentation of "positive images," its conscientious balancing of men and women
onscreen, and its assertion of human dignity for gays and
lesbians. In one sense of the term, the film is liberal because
it is not "conservative": it offers a much more tolerant and
affirming image of gay and lesbian life than the one circulated by the Right at the time. In another sense of the term,
the film is liberal because it is not "radical": it insists on a
single-issue, humanistic approach to the problems faced by
gay men and lesbians in the US, and it does not offer analysis
of the root causes of this group's oppression. In many ways,
"liberal" is a relative term, defined in contrast to other positions. Like most political labels, it is always in danger of
opportunistic and imprecise uses.

Liberalism classically refers to a cluster of philosophical
and ideological positions that insist on the primacy of individual liberty and equality. As a political philosophy, it is
associated with the bourgeois revolutions of the eighteenth

Definition of "a liberal"

88

century, which replaced top-down aristocratic and monarchic forms of government with more democratic ones, and which replaced pre-capitalist economic systems with privatized, market-based ones. Two primary texts of the liberal tradition are the US Constitution and the French *Déclaration des droits de l'homme et du citoyen* (*Declaration of the Rights of Man and of the Citizen*). I argue that *Word Is Out* is the quintessentially gay liberal film because it formally and ideologically presents gay and lesbian subjects in ways that are akin to how these documents define the proper citizen of liberal democracy.

Marxist theorists, beginning with Karl Marx, argue that the primary function of liberal ideology ("political liberalism") is to justify and naturalize the egoistic subject of capitalism ("economic liberalism"). They insist that political and economic liberalism have marched in lockstep from the beginning, long before current regimes of "neoliberalism" rendered the relationship between the two more explicit. In an analysis of the French *Déclaration*, Marx examines the distinction between the selfless citizen and the self-interested capitalist. He argues that the bourgeois revolution constructed a separation of spheres: on the one hand, there is the public sphere, where the "citizen" engages in "politics," and on the other hand, there is the private sphere of "civil society," where the individual actor (or simply "man" in the terminology of the *Déclaration*) participates in the new market economy. In this separation of the political from the

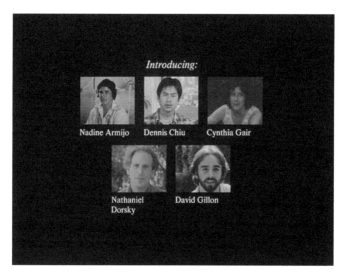

FIGURE 15. A series of isolated monads. DVD still.

economic, and of the social from the individual, "man" is refashioned not as a communal being (or in Marx's term, a "species-being"), but instead as an "isolated monad" driven by material self-interest. In the liberal public sphere, the egoistic subject of capitalism claims to act out of concern for and in concert with others, and yet it is precisely through the liberal discourse of inalienable rights that the individualism and self-centeredness motivating capitalism and the system of private property are naturalized (Marx 1843, 41–46).

Marx points out that the French *Déclaration* defines liberty as "the power which man has to do everything which does not harm the rights of others." He goes on to say that, "The limits within which each individual can act without harming others are determined by law, just as the boundary between two fields is marked by a stake … [L]iberty as a right of man is not founded upon the relations between man and man, but rather upon the separation of man from man. It is the right of such separation. The right of the circumscribed individual, withdrawn into himself" (ibid., 42). Political theorist Wendy Brown builds on Marx's critique of liberal rights discourse. She points out that rights in liberal democracy are usually negative rather than positive: e.g., freedom *from* discrimination, rather than the right *to*, say, housing. "The motion of rights is to push away or push away from—*against* others, *against* the state, *against* incursions, limitations, or encroachments upon our autonomy. Insofar as rights operate to distance and demarcate, they are a means of socially organizing us by separating us, using the fiction of our autonomy and independence to produce a social order reflecting it" (1995, 158).

Rights "from" vs. "to"

Like the French *Déclaration*, *Word Is Out* is at pains to construct a community of individuals, and it does so by presenting an illusion of civic participation and national community that is in fact an editing together of distinct cells, or "isolated monads." These cells are laterally distributed and presented as interchangeable, as if one could replace the subjects with a random sampling of twenty other lesbians and gay men and still have basically the same film—the same

Subjects as representative sample

collective portrait of good, rights-worthy subjects. *Word Is Out* downplays differences among queer populations, in particular between lesbians and gay men, as well as between queer and straight populations. And it does so largely by pushing particularities, such as political beliefs and sexual practices, off screen. By de-particularizing its subjects, the film universalizes gay and lesbian experience and renders it abstract. *Word Is Out* is bound up with the liberal separation of spheres in the sense that its main political project is to render homosexuality a nonpolitical issue, i.e., the purview of the individual rather than the citizen. The film articulates homosexuality not as a disruptive public force, as in gay-liberationist formulations, but as a bounded, privatized attribute. It seeks to make gay and lesbian life fit into an already dominant and naturalized liberal framework of understanding, one that passes as common sense in the US and thus need never justify or explain itself.

Marx's analysis is not the only understanding of liberalism circulating on the Left. Another position, articulated by Hannah Arendt (1951) and Giorgio Agamben (1998), insists that liberal democracy grants rights to some, its "citizens," only on condition of denying rights to others. This analysis urges us to look beyond the boundaries of *Word Is Out* for forms of 1970s queer life that were relegated offscreen and denied inclusion in the film's vision of gay and lesbian citizenship. One finds a very different approach in recent writing by political philosophers Jacques Rancière (2006) and

Slavoj Žižek (2007), who have sought to rethink liberal democracy more generously. Rancière insists that the universal and the particular are always in tension in the democratic project. Rather than insist that liberalism's profession of the universal rights of man is merely a ruse that masks the actual hegemony of particular interests (capitalists and private-property owners), he asks us to think about how the concept and rhetoric of universalism as it circulates in liberalism, ruse or not, enables those who are particularized through stigma and exploitation to imagine themselves as universal subjects and to begin making political demands for the rights that are denied them (2006, 51–70). This analysis encourages us to *liberalism/* think about how *Word Is Out* bears witness to a coming-into- *universal* universal-subjecthood of gays and lesbians in the US, after years of enduring the particularizing experiences of stigma, repression, and persecution. However one approaches the politics of the film, all of these critiques insist that liberalism is not merely a political orientation—certainly not simply a synonym for "pro-gay rights"—but that it fundamentally shapes how lesbians and gay men understand themselves and how they live their lives. Toward the end of the 1970s, gay men and lesbians in the US were under intense pressure to undo the social and political ruptures of the late 1960s and early 1970s, and to become proper liberal subjects.

M IS FOR MIRROR

Mirrors pop up surprisingly often in 1970s documentaries. They are frequently positioned to reflect the image of the camera (and the camera operator) back into the lens, thereby revealing the active role of the filmmaker and equipment in shaping a film's content. This technique works against the common practice in interview films of removing all visual and auditory traces of the filmmaker so that the interview subjects' statements seem spontaneous and self-generated. In his 1983 essay "The Voice of Documentary," Bill Nichols argues that interview films too often hand over the work of analysis entirely to their onscreen subjects, to the point of losing any "voice" of their own, which is to say their own argument and perspective on the historical and political issues they raise. He finds this loss of voice to be particularly troubling when films present subjects whose understanding of the issues raised is evidently incomplete or inadequate. Interview films often evince a naïve faith in the testimony of ordinary people, as if insightful political analysis will arise magically from their simple act of recounting their lives. Self-reflexive devices like mirrors, offscreen voice, and title cards can function to bring the filmmaker's perspective on particular themes (or on a particular subject's testimony) into the picture.

Along with a number of other Left documentary critics,

Nichols praises filmmaker Emile de Antonio as someone who overcame the limitations of the interview film by finding ways to infuse the form with critical reflexivity (1983, 56–58).[28] In his films, de Antonio does not present interview subjects as the bearers of complete and unequivocal truth. He regularly makes his own presence felt as an investigator who is actively trying to piece together meaning from fragments of history and testimony. In the 1976 film *Underground*, made with Haskell Wexler and Mary Lampson, de Antonio interviews members of the Weather Underground in a safe house. In a particularly famous shot, which recurs throughout the film, we see a mirror image of the group members' backs with the filmmakers' faces and camera visible beyond them. Although the filmmakers ostensibly designed the shot to maintain secrecy about the members' current appearances, there are less formally contrived ways to accomplish this; indeed, elsewhere in the film gauzy fabric, silhouetting, and a blurred lens do the same trick. The shot with the mirror functions more importantly as a way to reveal the presence of the filmmakers, to show that they are grappling with what they are hearing and that they are struggling with the question of violence and the end of the sixties.

At the other end of the spectrum from de Antonio, Nichols

---

28. See also Kahana (2008, 196–204); Kellner and Streible (2000); and Waugh (1976).

FIGURE 16. The mirror as reflexivity: filming the Weather Underground in Emile de Antonio's *Underground* (1976). DVD still. Copyright Turin Film Corporation, courtesy of Sphinx Productions.

lumps *Word Is Out* with films that he criticizes for lacking "voice" (1983, 56–59). On the surface, it is strange that Nichols puts *Word Is Out* in this group, as the film includes many ostensibly self-reflexive devices, which would seem to indicate either that it is a more savvy film than Nichols gives it credit for, or else that it includes these devices but does not use them critically. Just after the opening credits of *Word Is Out*, we encounter a shot that looks a lot like *Underground*. Roger Harkenrider sits in front of a huge studio mirror in which we see reflections of Peter Adair at the camera and Rob Epstein recording sound (later in the film Adair and Epstein trade places). A smaller mirror, positioned for the same effect, hangs above the couch during the joint inter-

Strategic + intentional reflective style

FIGURE 17. The mirror as simple reflection?: filming Roger Harkenrider at his acting studio in *Word Is Out*. DVD still.

view with Pam Jackson and Rusty Millington; here we see Nancy Adair at the camera. Moving from mirrors into the codes of documentary reflexivity more broadly, there are a score of moments in *Word Is Out* that seem designed to remind us that a film is being made. In certain shots we see the filmmakers; in others we hear their voices; and in still others we watch and listen as the making of the film and its politics of inclusion are discussed by or with the interview subjects.

The introductory sequence of the film contains more apparently self-reflexive moments than any other comparable-length segment. Here, Nancy Adair accidentally asks Elsa Gidlow how old she was when she was born; Betty Powell points out that she cannot single-handedly stand in for all black lesbians; Mark Pinney insists that gay conservatives are "damn important" too; and Nathaniel Dorsky fumbles for words and then asks if the camera is still running. In this short four-minute sequence we hear three of the six filmmakers ask offscreen questions. Perhaps most stunning is the very first shot, when Veronica Selver asks Nadine Armijo, "Were you—Were you always gay?" In Armijo's awkward and faltering response we witness her identity and personal narrative come together in service of the film's normative project: "Always? Hmm ... I don't think so. Well maybe ... I don't know. It's hard to say. I think I ... Yeah, I've been gay." To which Selver then asks, "When did you discover it?"

By front-loading such moments, the film seems eager to establish something quickly; and it is probably not that the narrative of born-this-way homosexuality is a construct, or that the filmmakers are actively shaping the testimony of the interview subjects. According to Nancy Adair, the film includes moments that reveal the filmmakers' presence in order to provide the viewer with a point of identification during the interviews, so that it seems less like listening to a monologue and more like participating in a conversation (1978, 283). Along the same lines, it seems to be by design that the filmmakers come across in these moments as fallible, everyday people: we hear them flubbing and searching

A dialogue

for words more often than we hear them confidently giving direction. By foregrounding the casual rapport between the filmmakers and their interview subjects, and even at times the non-professionalism of the shoots, what seem at first like "reflexive" moments instead become the opposite. Rather than promoting a critical distance from the film and from its construction of the "truth" of gay lives, these moments take us behind the scenes to convince us that the film is *not* ~~Unscripted~~ a carefully manipulated representation of reality. They invite us to enter uncritically into the film's chain of affirming identifications.

N IS FOR NARRATIVE

> These autobiographies will be inherently dramatic because
> the process of coming out itself is dramatic. It is the story
> of human struggle and human victory.
> —Peter Adair, in his 1974 proposal for the film, then titled
> "Coming Out"

> Less noticeably but more devastatingly hampering the
> film's intelligibility is its lack of societal vision and inter-
> pretation. The many faces and the many stories are not
> organized into a structure that amounts to anything. Like
> pieces in a misassembled picture puzzle, they go together
> to form another problem, mystification instead of com-
> munication.
> —Ray Olson, in a 1979 article discussing *Word Is Out*

A number of reviewers expressed confusion about the organization of *Word Is Out*.[29] There seems to be a strong premise for the first part of the film, "Part One: The Early Years."
Here we encounter mainly older (mid-thirties and up) gay
men and lesbians who recount their experiences before gay
liberation. The structuring principles behind "Part Two:
Growing Up" and "Part Three: From Now On" are less

---

29. See for instance Atwell (1978, 52); Bronski (1978); and Olson
(1979, 10).

clear. Much of the trouble, felt even in the titles of the three parts, arises from the film's effort to merge biography with collective history: *Word Is Out* tries to map the developmental narrative of the gay individual onto the developmental narrative of gay people as a whole. As such, "Part One: The Early Years" not only presents gay men and lesbians who came of age before Stonewall; it is also meant to represent a stage in the lives of all gays and lesbians: the unhappy period of the closet and self-hatred before coming into self-awareness (Part Two) and then coming out (Part Three). Things start to get muddled when the interviewees of Part One reappear in the later parts, as they too have "grown up" and entered the post-Stonewall present, and similarly when those interviewees introduced in Part Two proceed to recount their childhood, pre-out experiences.

At the level of individual life narratives, the three-part structure generally takes this form: first, one's life before coming into self-awareness as gay or lesbian; second, one's entrance into self-acceptance and relationships with other gay people; and third, one's exposure and risk as an "out" person in the straight world. At the level of the collective historical narrative, the three-part structure generally takes this form: first, the experiences of gay men and lesbians before gay liberation and the woman's movement, including tales of oppressive straight marriages and forced institutionalization; second, the experiences of a new generation of gay men and lesbians who have come of age after Stonewall and

Handwritten margin notes:

I Closet

II Awareness

III Acceptance

Most Muddled

Or III as Out
↑
Individual

Group
↓
Historical

I Pre-Stonewall

II After Stonewall

III Future

who do not seem to suffer from the same problems or hang-ups as earlier generations; and third, a collective assertion of self-worth as lesbians and gay men move toward increased social acceptance. There is also ambivalence in this third act. It is here that Pat Bond expresses nostalgia for an earlier time when one felt "the adventure of being different in a straight world."

The film's preference for certain forms of gay and lesbian life over others becomes clearest in Part Two, which concerns the individual's transitional stage between being in the closet (Part One) and being out (Part Three). Being out is defined in the film as engaging with the straight world as an openly gay person.[30] In Part Two, the gay subject who has recently entered into a gay or lesbian community—but who has not yet come out—builds up self-respect (this is the most affirming part of the film) and comes to understand what constitutes a proper gay awakening and a proper gay relationship. At the end of this section, we encounter the film's representatives of a new generation of lesbians and gay men. Linda Marco and Cynthia Gair tell giddy stories of first lesbian love that are marked by a G-rated, adolescent

Awakening to love— innocent

30. How else could we hope to understand Nancy Adair's question to Pat Bond, "Have you ever come out of the closet?," which is asked near the end of the film after it has already been established that Bond has taken part in a vibrant lesbian community since World War II? Bond replies, "Yeah, a couple, three times. I'm coming out now, right? Big white face on the screen saying, 'Yeah, I'm gay.'"

awkwardness, and Nick Dorsky and David Gillon say that their discovery of the capacity to love another person has legitimized them as human beings. The achievement of a loving relationship—importantly, one that need not be sexual—is presented here as both a humanizing experience and the ultimate step in "growing up."

It is also in Part Two that we hear of explicitly political organizations for the first time: Michael Mintz speaks of "the Alliance" at Princeton, Gair talks of meeting a woman at a Radicalesbians gathering, and Sally Gearhart mentions Gay Women's Liberation. However, these organizations come across as little more than support groups and sites for social and romantic networking. No political agenda is presented in the film beyond the liberal one of working toward social (Political) acceptance within a larger society that one does not seek to change. The film's narrative problems are inseparable from act its liberal conflation of gay politics with the act of coming Act of out. For gay liberalism, visibility is the means; equality is coming out the end. Coming out *is* the political act, upon completion of which gay and lesbian politics should, ideally, cease to exist. End of Because of this structuring liberal fantasy, *Word Is Out* falters most in its third section, as it labors to infuse its vision gay politics of openly gay life with either narrative impetus or political energy. The section title, "From Now On," suggests neither agency, in the form of a call to action, nor more changes ahead—nor even that more changes *should* lie ahead.

O IS FOR OUT

Most gay and lesbian films before the late 1970s took it for granted that the truth of gay and lesbian experience did not lie waiting on the surface of the world. Visible, natural-light "reality" was the realm of the closeted life, of deceptive self-presentation. How could a vérité camera, non-interventionist and restricted to the surface of things, hope to capture the truth that hid from view? As such, early gay and lesbian films—from the mid-century avant-garde to the 1970s "performative documentaries" discussed in "D Is for Documentary"—made heavy use of theatrical contrivance, as well as a general camp flamboyance, to conjure hidden truths for the camera: an exteriorization of inner fantasies and desires, a publicization of secret communities, and a realization of hitherto unrealized (and often, beyond the space of the film's production, still impossible to realize) queer realities. At the same time, the performers' onscreen flamboyance was an act of resistance to day-to-day mandates of passing, conformity, and non-publicity for queer people. In this way, the early films evinced a non-liberal understanding of out gay life: they envisioned coming out as a first step toward dramatic transformation of the self and (ideally) society, and they took it for granted that performances of straightness, sameness, and respectability would not follow a person beyond the closet door.

Coming Out as the Start [handwritten marginalia]

The passing experience, with its training in double vision and divided self-performance, was arguably the critical edge and formal engine of early gay and lesbian filmmaking.[31] By contrast, *Word Is Out* articulates a vision of gay and lesbian experience that is no longer riven by conflicts of surface and depth, public and private, light and shadow. In the film's sunlit gay present, after both the closeted youth of the individual and the benighted pre-Stonewall past of gay men and lesbians as a group, there is only wholeness and non-contradiction. By the logic of gay liberalism, coming out is the coming into self-honesty, into political legitimacy, and into unadorned and unremarkable documentary realism. This vision of an undivided gay self is then extended back, paradoxically, into pre-out gay life. For gay liberalism, coming out is about gay people finding the courage to speak up about who they already are, and about making straight people realize that they already know gay people and that they are basically the same as themselves. One comes out not with a sense of excitement, but with a sigh of relief.

Although liberationist and cultural-feminist currents are felt in *Word Is Out*, the film's structuring form is liberal. The film was designed so that it would not scare off either closeted gay people or phobic straight people, and for this reason

31. See Babuscio (1978) for an articulation of the "passing experience" and a discussion of its link to camp and theatricality in gay film culture.

FIGURE 18. The 1977 San Francisco Gay Freedom Day parade as presented in *Word Is Out*. DVD still.

[handwritten margin note: Focus on individual vs. group]

it articulates coming out as a largely non-disruptive act for both self and society. So even though a push toward the exterior drives *Word Is Out*—shaped as it is around a formal, narrative, and ideological program of coming out—it is no accident that the film's focus is resignedly inward, on individual people and couples in intimate settings.

The contradictions underlying the film's vision of outness are felt most in those moments when it presents public gay political activity, especially the shots toward the end of the film and in the closing credits that feature the 1977 San

FIGURE 19. The same parade as presented in Arthur Bressan's *Gay USA* (1978). DVD still. Courtesy of Frameline and the estate of Arthur Bressan.

Francisco Gay Freedom Day parade. To get this footage, Peter Adair stationed himself high up in the bed of a truck parked along the parade route. As a result, the images are from a distance and at a high angle. The marchers appear in shallow focus and are framed from the chest or neck up; individuals are flattened into the crowd and become difficult to distinguish from each other. The footage gives the impression that the people who showed up for the city's first Gay Pride march after Anita Bryant's victory in Dade

County were no more diverse, perhaps even less so, than the selection of gay men and lesbians interviewed in the film. By way of comparison, Arthur Bressan's 1978 film *Gay USA* (which is discussed more in "U Is for USA") presents footage from the same parade. The film combines aerial shots with street-level photography, and it has a particular fondness for low-angle shots taken close to the ground at the very heart of the parade, so that we see marchers streaming by us on the right and the left. The camera weaves in and out of the crowd. It also pulls both the visually ordinary and the visually extraordinary—drag queens, marchers in agitprop costumes, others in purely festive get-ups—to the sidelines for extended interviews and lengthier shots. Although the two films are in many respects complementary, *Gay USA* demonstrates the range and rowdiness of the 1977 Gay Freedom Day parade—and of gay and lesbian politics at the time of Anita Bryant—to an extent that *Word Is Out* does not. From Bressan's film, viewers get a sense of the disruptive potential of out gay life.

Non-threatening

P IS FOR POSITIVE IMAGES

> We could have made a terrible film using twenty-six gay
> people and it still would have been taken to represent
> who gay people are. So we had to approach that problem
> responsibly. [...] And that's a fundamental problem because
> the initial temptation is to use people who are role models,
> who are acceptable—which means you are adopting the
> values of the enemy. Now on the other hand, you don't
> want to use all drag queens. And I'm not personally from
> the John Rechy school of 'Well, fuck 'em. We'll screw in
> the streets and that's the revolution.' That's not my par-
> ticular way. So what do you do?
> —Peter Adair, in a 1978 interview with Vito Russo

As with coming out, the call to record and disseminate
"positive images" is often associated with more assimilationist, liberal tendencies in gay and lesbian activism. However,
just as the understanding of coming out varied considerably
among liberals and liberationists, so too the idea of what
a positive image was or should be was a site of profound
contestation. Whether or not they were of "the John Re-
chy school," all practitioners of positive-image filmmaking
found themselves faced with a sticky ontological riddle: any
call for "positive images" was caught in a tension between
depicting "things as they are" and "things as they should
be" (Waldman 1978). Or as Richard Dyer alternately put

Positive:
1. there
2. good
3. real

it, adding a third variable to the mix: "Positive meant three, not altogether compatible things: thereness, insisting on the fact of our existence; goodness, asserting our worth and that of our life-styles; and realness, showing what we were in fact like" (Dyer 1990, 274). In some ways fiction films, avant-garde works, and performative documentaries had an easier time of things than realist documentaries because the former could present clearly utopian and fantastical imagery without contradiction. Realist documentaries, beholden to an ideal of authenticity and more reliant on the indexical properties of celluloid to legitimate their truth claims, had to find ways to represent lesbians and gay men "positively" despite all the evidence that the group lived negatively—experiencing persecution, ostracism, loneliness, depression, self-hatred, and so on.

Respectability w/in gay community

There is a tension throughout *Word Is Out* between the aim of affirmation and the aim of representation. The former is an inherently valorizing impulse that privileges certain forms of gay and lesbian life over others, while the latter presents a non-hierarchical array of gay and lesbian experience and insists that the refusal of hierarchy is in itself something to value. In Part Three of the film, George Mendenhall makes the statement that for twenty-five years he has had sexual encounters, "occasional pick-ups," without emotional intimacy. The film even grants him space to defend the practice, in response to Peter Adair's offscreen query, "Do you think that's healthy?" Yet Mendenhall's defense of promiscuity here, like his defense of intergenerational relationships in Part One, feels like an aberrant position within a film that clearly valorizes sustained couple relationships. Although Peter Adair, in the above epigraph, expresses a wariness of "role models," it is not hard to determine which aspects of gay and lesbian life the film valorizes as good, and which ones bad. One of the ways the film resolves the tension between affirmation and representation is by aligning "negative" qualities and practices with the older generation and "positive" ones with the younger generation. In this way, things like cruising older men and anonymous sex are included in the film, but they become part of the gay past or leftover practices from an earlier generation.

Past —
negative
Present/
Future —
positive

From my perspective, the older men and women in *Word Is Out* are fascinating and engaging subjects. They tell stories about their pasts that are alternately funny and tragic, and they express an array of refreshingly distinct perspectives on gay and lesbian life. They are also at times cantankerous, bizarre, even annoying. It is in relation to them that I can appreciate the filmmakers' insistence that *Word Is Out* redefined the "positive image," so that it was no longer about presenting people who are acceptable or even necessarily likable, but instead about presenting people who are "self-affirmed" and "self-actualized" (Mariposa Film Group 1978, 9; N. Adair 1978, 297). Each of the interview subjects from the older generation is a survivor.

By contrast, I find the young people in the film to be

rather bland; they lack the charisma and narrative interest of their onscreen elders. In a 1978 interview with the film-makers, DuMont Howard and Jeffrey Escoffier say that they feel the same way: "the older people stole the show." In response, Rob Epstein says that when he and the other film-makers screened the first rough cut (which featured eight interview subjects, seven of them stand-outs from Part One), a lot of the feedback was that the film was too negative, that it contained too many "heavy experiences." "So with a lot of the younger people we went after … we were looking for people who felt good about being gay, whose experience was pleasant and easy and who could tell nice stories about it" (Mariposa Film Group 1978, 10). Lucy Massie Phenix follows his point by noting that the early interviews were more open-ended than the later ones; in the later shoots the filmmakers had less film and a clearer sense of where they wanted to take each interview (ibid., 11). Perhaps it is for these reasons, pertaining mainly to the order and circumstances in which the interviews were conducted, that the generational divide seems so strong. As Epstein suggests, what is positive about the younger people is that they are happy about being gay. They do not speak of much trauma (though Michael Mintz recounts narrowly escaping a gay bashing), nor do they express particularly rich ideas about lesbian or gay consciousness. They are positive role models mainly because they lack the characteristics that the film has called into question through its treatment of the testimony

112

FIGURE 20. The Save Our Human Rights group marching in the 1977 San Francisco Gay Freedom Day parade. Photograph by Crawford Barton. Courtesy of the GLBT Historical Society.

of the older subjects: no one among the younger generation is butch, separatist, cross-age desiring, or promiscuous.

In this respect, the film's presentation of young people takes the form of what we might think of as *the non-negative image*: the image that is considered positive not so much because it possesses good qualities, but because it lacks "bad" ones. This approach became particularly salient during the battle with Anita Bryant and John Briggs over gay rights. The best example is perhaps the Save Our Human Rights group, whose representatives appeared *en bloc* at the 1977 Gay Freedom Day parade in San Francisco, waving American flags and clad in matching white T-shirts that simply stated "Save Our Human Rights." Constituting a sea of sameness, they sought to make a spectacle of their non-spectacularity and thereby shift mainstream news media coverage of the parade away from the less straight-friendly images marching farther down the line, i.e., the drag queens and the half-naked men. The group's message was a popular one, and signs carrying the same slogan appeared all over the parade that year. Nevertheless, the group's members marched to a different drummer than the many gay and lesbian activists who had spent the decade fostering, valorizing, and publicizing queer difference.

[handwritten margin note: Alienating vs. relating]

Q IS FOR QUEER

Word Is Out is a rigorously "gay and lesbian" film: half of its participants are identified as gay men and half are identified as lesbian women, both in front of and behind the camera. This is not to say that the film never presents bisexual or transgender experiences, or that nothing about the film is ~~Broad~~ "queer." In the mid- to late-1970s, "gay" and "lesbian" were ~~terms~~ rather flexible terms—arguably more so than they are now— with blurred boundaries around the identities they sought to fix and describe. Many bisexual and transgender experiences circulated under these signs. At the same time, the terms were under intense definitional pressure, both from within and from without lesbian and gay male spaces. I have used the terms "gay" and "lesbian" throughout this book because they are the labels with which the film and its makers defined themselves; however, I have tried to avoid letting the terms consolidate and reduce to the narrower senses by which we often understand them today. There is certainly a need to distinguish bisexual, transgender, and other categories of identification and experience from gay and lesbian in order to resist the ways that the latter frequently colonize and render invisible the former, but there is also something to be gained by remembering what gay and lesbian were before LGBT and before queer.

Word Is Out shares in a widespread 1970s ethos that

valorized androgyny as the ideal for both male- and female-bodied gender expression. The embrace of androgyny opened up gay and lesbian identities and communities to alternate experiences of gender; at the same time, androgyny often became a norm in its own right. Among the film's gay male subjects, *Word Is Out* showcases poet and activist Tede Mathews as an androgynous, genderqueer man. With his teddy bear at his side and a "Capitalism is Dying" flyer pinned to the wall behind him, he explains the absurdity of gender norms and contributes the proto-queer-theoretical point that "we're all born naked, and anything anybody wears at any time is drag." Mathews is central to the film's larger case on behalf of male effeminacy. Filmmaker Andrew Brown told me that a number of gay men who saw the film, both at pre-screenings and after it was released, objected that it contained too many sissy boys and faggots, too many stereotypes of male homosexuality with which they did not want to be associated. Apparently Roger Harkenrider's inclusion, as one of the film's more exuberant personalities, was a particularly hot-button issue. Brown himself appears briefly onscreen with one of the film's many sensitive men (and his lover at the time): the red-headed Freddy Gray.

At the same time that *Word Is Out* uses Mathews to queer gay male masculinity, the film carefully distinguishes his gender expression from less androgynous models of both transsexuality and drag. We learn in Part Two that Mathews no longer identifies as transsexual—"I always felt that I

FIGURE 21. Tede Mathews teaches radical gender theory to the film's makers and viewers. DVD still.

was a girl trapped in a boy's body." "Do you still feel that?" "No."—and also that his experience of drag has moved away from an early identification with passive female roles to an identification with strong women and a more fluid gender presentation. In this way, however much androgyny opened things up for gay men in the 1970s, it was also used to police the boundaries of acceptable gender expression.

In her book *Transgender History*, Susan Stryker presents the 1970s as a particularly "difficult" decade, when a series of political and cultural developments resulted in a separating

FIGURE 22. Good femme, bad butch: Pam Jackson listens as Rusty Millington talks apologetically about male identification. DVD still.

Intersection of gender + sex

out of transgender identities and activism from both lesbian and gay male formations (2008, 91–120). Among her examples, Stryker discusses the marginalization of female-bodied, masculine-identified people within many lesbian communities at the time. The 1970s tension between butchness and androgyny is felt in some of the film's scenes with Rusty Millington. In its presentation of Millington's testimony, the film first establishes her earlier male identification and then makes it clear that she has since learned the error of her ways. Interestingly, a similar narrative appeared in Peter

Adair's original proposal for the film, which he drafted in 1974 before any shooting had begun. The proposal includes three fictional interview transcripts, each of them projections of the content Adair hoped to find when he conducted his documentary interviews. The third one, entitled "Being Open," presents a butch lesbian who, after being abandoned by her lover, leaves suburbia to live on a farm with two liberated women and begins to take tentative steps away from male identification: "I also have had to learn to do housework and other things I wouldn't have dreamed of doing. I think I'm a lot more myself now … Don't tell them, but I still like chopping wood or even shoveling manure better than washing dishes" (P. Adair 1974, 11).[32]

Although the film makes a point to valorize androgyny in opposition to butchness, drag, and transsexuality, it is important to recognize that it also clears space for a reevaluation of these experiences and identifications within a context that was often hostile toward them. Mathews' statements about drag, however qualified, serve to defend and recuperate the practice from widespread feminist critiques of

[handwritten margin notes: Andro / Butch / Drag / Trans]

---

32. *Word Is Out* balances its 1970s embrace of androgyny with a liberal investment in passing and gender normativity. This helps to explain why the film is so concerned about Millington's butchness, yet shows no parallel investment in disabusing Pam Jackson of her femme identification, which in one sequence even includes a *Playboy* half-shirt.

it as an inherently misogynist practice.[33] Similarly, Jackson and Millington are not included in the film simply so that Millington can be trained out of her butchness (a project of dubious success, at best). The film's inclusion of the undeniably likeable couple speaks back to second-wave feminism's delegitimization of butch/femme ways of life.

The film's relationship to bisexuality is similarly complex and contradictory. On one hand, *Word Is Out* seems eager to essentialize and compartmentalize same-sex desire, and it includes no one who explicitly identifies as bisexual. On the other hand, the film includes a number of subjects who have come out of earlier heterosexual relationships and who do not disavow these relationships as the results of a closeted life or false consciousness (though admittedly a number of them do). A few of the film's participants would later enter into heterosexual relationships again. For instance, the "Afterthoughts" special feature on the thirtieth-anniversary

Handwritten margin notes: "definition of a woman"; "Bisexual / pansexual / queer ↓ There are so many labels today"

---

33. As such, the scenes with Mathews should be thought about alongside the film's other, more circumspect representations of drag: George Mendenhall's emotional discussion of José Sarria's proto-gay-liberation drag performances and group sing-alongs at San Francisco's Black Cat bar in the 1950s, a brief shot of a drag cheerleader rallying the crowd during the fourth annual San Francisco Police vs. Gays softball game, and an almost subliminal shot of a flaming queen marching in a Pride parade. This last image is flashed as an example of the type of flamboyant gay behavior that makes conservative businessman Mark Pinney so nervous.

DVD includes Cynthia Gair's discussion of her shifting desire and her current relationship with a man.

Lucy Massie Phenix was married to a man she loved when she made *Word Is Out*. As she worked on the film project, she learned to valorize her lesbianism without disavowing her heterosexuality. In a statement solicited for possible inclusion in the accompanying book to the film, she wrote:

> I am not only gay ... I became open to the possibility
> of my own homosexuality and I celebrated that
> I became larger and could experience more as a
> growing human being, as a more self-aware woman.
> And now I am unable and unwilling, if I am to be
> honest with myself, to label myself gay ONLY when
> I feel a strong and loving connection with both the
> men and the women I have loved, do love, will love. I
> feel more and more gay in my sensibilities, more and
> more lesbian in my commitments, more and more
> open, bisexual if you insist, in my sexual, physical
> expression of caring for the people I love, women and
> men. (Adair Papers, box 14, folder 9)

In another statement, which was included in the accompanying book, Massie Phenix says that she sees the film as part of a larger cultural push for human beings to move beyond the separation between male and female and the division between gay and straight (N. Adair 1978, 311). While some viewers see *Word Is Out* as a film that presents fixed

More beyond the binary

definitions of gay and lesbian, there is nothing to prevent others from seeing it as the opposite: a film that celebrates a queer openness to change and possibility.

R IS FOR RETROVIRAL

In a special feature of the thirtieth-anniversary DVD of *Word Is Out*, Rick Stokes discusses the impact of AIDS on the gay male community in San Francisco. Images of the film's interview subjects who died of AIDS appear on the screen as he speaks: Donald Hackett, Tede Mathews, Michael Mintz, and Stokes' own lover, David Clayton. Stokes talks about AIDS with the same devastating Midwestern openness and steady passion with which his younger self discusses family betrayal and shock treatments in the film.

Watching *Word Is Out* today, across three decades of the intervening AIDS crisis, we are compelled to view it differently from its original viewers. Although AIDS is now a global pandemic, mainstream cultural discourse in the US often relegates memory of the disease to the decade and a half stretching from the first signs in 1981 to the appearance of protease inhibitors and powerful new drug cocktails in the mid-1990s. As HIV/AIDS became "manageable" for those with access to the new treatments, many activists breathed a sigh of relief and turned their attention to a renewed gay-rights agenda, one increasingly preoccupied with marriage and the military. When AIDS is discussed today, it is often as an apolitical tragedy that took the lives of many of our civil rights pioneers, such as Peter Adair. However, this is not the only way to understand the relationship between AIDS and the history of gay politics. Especially before the mid-1990s, the AIDS crisis fundamentally challenged gay liberal understandings of privacy, visibility, sex, and the political, and prompted a renewed radicalism for many lesbians and gay men. Gay liberalism's inability to speak candidly about gay male sexual culture was a major roadblock for AIDS activism as it sought to promote safer sex and to remove social stigma from people with AIDS. The crisis compelled cultural activists, including Adair, who had earlier promoted tolerance by dissociating gays and lesbians from stigmatized practices to now find ways to talk about these practices openly and non-judgmentally, even positively (Crimp 1987).

Before his death in 1996, Adair created two major films related to the epidemic as well as a number of shorter informational works for use in HIV/AIDS clinics. With Rob Epstein, he made *The AIDS Show* (1986), a documentary presentation of one of the first stage productions about AIDS (Blaney 2011). Then, on his own as director (with Janet Cole producing and Veronica Selver editing), he made *Absolutely Positive* (1991), a film that reworks the template of *Word Is Out* for the AIDS crisis.[34] The film cuts together

34. For his part, Epstein also directed, along with Jeffrey Friedman, *Common Threads: Stories from the Quilt* (1989), an Academy-Award-winning documentary that presents a series of profiles of people represented by panels in the NAMES Project AIDS Memorial Quilt. For an account of Epstein's career since *Word Is Out*, see Hays (2007, 99–111).

FIGURE 23. Peter Adair turns the camera on himself at the end of
Absolutely Positive (1991). DVD still. Courtesy of Haney Armstrong.

interviews with eleven people who are HIV-positive and living asymptomatically. Notably, Adair appears in *Absolutely
Positive* alongside the official cast. For most of the film we
see him only obliquely, made aware of his presence mainly
through the voiceover track. However, in the film's final shot
he is fully, visually present. Turning from his word proces-
sor to face us and the camera, he says that if they found a
cure tomorrow, part of him, ironically, would be depressed
because he's worked so hard to accept being HIV-positive.
He concludes, "I'd get over it though."

Designed to be shown on PBS, *Absolutely Positive* is by no means visually explicit about sex or drugs, but these subjects infuse the film as we witness person after person discussing openly and without shame the various ways they contracted the virus. Like *Word Is Out*, the film's main purpose is to humanize a population whose members are both stigmatized and isolated from each another. Also like the earlier film, it presents its central topic for the most part as an individual, non-political issue, and it keeps its various interview subjects restricted to their respective frames. At the same time, as with *Word Is Out*, Adair's decisions in framing the project seem to have enabled it to reach a larger audience than would have been possible for a more formally experimental, politically radical, or sexually explicit film.[35]

Among the interview subjects of *Word Is Out*, Stokes comes closest to the candor of *Absolutely Positive* in his statements about sex. There is palpable joy in his recollections of childhood sex with other boys, as well as in the matter-

---

35. *Absolutely Positive* includes black gay filmmaker Marlon Riggs among its interview subjects. Riggs' 1989 film *Tongues Untied*, a performative documentary about black gay men that includes discussion of HIV/AIDS, aired on PBS's *POV* series the same season as *Absolutely Positive*. But while *Absolutely Positive* was aired by most of the country's PBS affiliates, two-thirds refused to show *Tongues Untied* (Gregg 1992). Riggs' film also became a lightning rod of the early 1990s "culture wars," as conservatives insisted that the film was pornographic and obscene and used it as a visual aid in their efforts to dismantle government funding of the arts.

of-fact way that he tells how "really good satisfying sex with a man" gave him the strength to refuse the traps of a bad straight marriage and a closeted life. However, these statements all occur early on, before the film introduces Clayton, at which point the two men are quickly absorbed into the film's overarching argument for long-term relationships (see "S Is for Settling Down"). Stokes' affirming relationship to sex is subtly made a thing of the past, associated with pre-Stonewall gay life.

Stokes and Clayton were not only romantic partners, they were also business partners. Along with a dozen other gay men, they founded the Ritch Street Health Club, which from the mid-1960s well into the 1970s was the preeminent gay men's bathhouse in San Francisco. It was elegantly appointed and offered a comfortable place for gay men to engage in sex free from police surveillance and persecution. The money from the baths funded Stokes' entrance into law and politics. It also helped finance *Word Is Out*. Stokes was a key early backer of the film and also introduced Peter Adair to potential funders among his circle of wealthy Bay Area lawyers and businessmen (N. Adair 1978, 284). Stokes was an important activist lawyer in the 1970s, and he helped and defended many gay men when they were arrested on morals charges for public sex. Although a rich culture of gay male sex funded and motivated Stokes' activism, he was silent about his involvement with the baths during his campaigns to enter political office. He is best known today as the gay

[handwritten margin note: Stokes as a backer]

man who ran against Harvey Milk for City Supervisor in 1977 and lost, an event that is often now memorialized as the moment when respectable, old-guard gay establishment politics (Stokes was backed in his campaign by conservative *Advocate* editor David Goodstein and Alice B. Toklas Democratic Club founder Jim Foster) gave way to Milk's new combination of youth-driven street activism and charm-driven deal-making. By the time *Word Is Out* appeared, Stokes had sold his interest in the Ritch Street Health Club. The bathhouse was purchased by the national Club Baths chain, which was owned by Miami businessman and gay activist Jack Campbell, who played a major role in the battle against Anita Bryant in Dade County.[36]

Gay male sexual culture played a significant part, then, not only in the backstory of *Word Is Out*, but in the course of 1970s gay politics more broadly, including the late-1970s struggles over gay rights. The twin forces of AIDS panic and gay-liberal respectability (then and now) have largely prevented us from seeing and remembering this.[37] Adair and

[handwritten margin note: Gay male sexual culture clash w/ respectability]

36. Much of the background on Stokes from this paragraph is taken from Clendinen and Nagourney (1999, 148–63 and 331–49). See also Shilts (1982, 169–85). For Campbell's role in the struggle against Bryant, see Fejes (2008).

37. For a discussion of gay bathhouses as well as other sexual cultures and practices that became sites of political contestation in the first two decades of the AIDS epidemic, see *Dangerous Bedfellows* (1996).

the other filmmakers shot footage inside a gay bathhouse, but it was one of the many vérité sequences that ended up on the cutting-room floor.

S IS FOR SETTLING DOWN

> I grew up with the expectation that someday I would meet
> somebody and I would fall in love with that person and get
> married and settle down.
> —David Clayton at the end of Part One of *Word Is Out*

Word Is Out is structured so that people whom we first meet
on their own reappear later as halves of couples, e.g., Nadine Armijo, Freddy Gray, Michael Mintz, and Rick Stokes.
Only John Burnside and Harry Hay are together onscreen
from the beginning. This technique is played to full effect in
the case of Pam Jackson and Rusty Millington, who are presented separately throughout Part One, but then appear together in Part Two as we hear their shared story of how they
met. Each of the film's three parts culminates in an implicit
argument for coupledom, as does the film as a whole. Part
One ends with the camera drawing back from Stokes' face
to reveal his partner of sixteen years, David Clayton, seated
at his side. Part Two draws to a close with the presentation
of Michael Mintz with Earl Carter and stories from a number of interview subjects about the awkwardness and thrill of
embarking on a first same-sex relationship. And Part Three
culminates in Nadine Armijo and Rosa Montoya seated together on their bed, the same bed that seemed so large and
empty when Armijo sat on it alone in the film's opening shot.

In a 1979 article that provides an analysis of seventeen

FIGURE 24. Individuals become couples: expanding the frame to show David Clayton seated beside Rick Stokes at the end of Part One. DVD still.

gay-produced and gay-themed films from the decade, Ray Olson criticizes *Word Is Out* for its overemphasis of couples, as well as for the ways its rhetorical and ideological project seems to hinge on showing straight America that "gays, too, are in the market for love" (10).[38] The film's pro-coupling, pro-romantic-love position can make it seem very relevant to today's marriage-rights movement. David Bohnett, who

---

38. For other critiques along this line, see Atwell (1978, 53) and Waugh (1977, 27).

funded the film's restoration, succinctly connects the film to gay marriage activism in a two-and-a-half minute bonus feature on the thirtieth-anniversary DVD. He explains to the camera, "The movie was the beginning of that process of coming into our own as a community of lesbians and gay men, enjoying freedoms that we have never enjoyed before. Today, thirty years later, we have made unbelievable strides. We have built on what began with the stories of the people in 1977 to where full equality is within our reach, within our lifetimes." The final forty seconds of the bonus feature present images of newlywed lesbian and gay couples exiting San Francisco City Hall during the brief period in 2004 when the county granted marriage licences to same-sex couples. These images are followed by three photographs of smiling gay families.

Many viewers today likely share Bohnett's appreciation of *Word Is Out* as a powerful testament to the resiliency of gay couples during an embattled moment in the nation's past. It was a time when few gay men and lesbians considered gay marriage a viable political cause: on the one hand, because liberal goals at the time were much more moderate (such as the basic workplace and housing antidiscrimination struggles against Bryant and Briggs), and on the other hand, because second-wave feminist critiques of the institution of marriage were still widespread and taken seriously. Visions of gay and lesbian existence that did not model themselves on heterosexual norms of coupling had not yet been pushed

132

underground. In this regard, it is interesting that there are no scenes in the film where any of the avowed lesbian feminists appear on camera with a lover. An exploration of their alternative relationship formations—or, for those who were part of committed couples, a discussion of how they balanced this with their political convictions—would have complicated the film's overarching argument for the couple form.

[handwritten margin note: lesbian feminist ≠ marriage?]

Watching and listening to the film closely, straight marriage establishes a stronger presence than gay marriage. The film's subjects are moving out of and away from the former more clearly than they can be understood, from today's vantage point, to be moving toward the latter. Particularly in Part One, conscripted heterosexual marriage seems to be the common trauma of the participants, more unifying than tales of shock therapy and workplace discrimination. The many negative associations with straight marriage, especially in this early section of the film, challenge the assumption that it is a ritual or institution that the interview subjects idealize or that they look to in order to give sense and structure to their current relationships.

Even Pam Jackson's statement in the final ten minutes of the film is more suspicious of "till death do us part" than a lot of the rhetoric coming out of today's marriage-rights movement. Jackson is deeply committed to Rusty Millington, but she is also aware of the unpredictability of life and desire. "If you'd asked me, eight years ago, if I was going

[handwritten margin note: Doubtful of marriage]

to be queer, if I was going to be living with a woman and give up my children or anything else, I'd have said you were a lousy liar. So now I say, only until tomorrow, because I will never say never again." And Millington, turning to the woman she will still be with more than thirty years later, adds: "Or forever."

T IS FOR THIRD WORLD GAY

At the end of *Word Is Out*, Dennis Chiu is shown marching in the 1977 San Francisco Gay Freedom Day parade
with a banner for the group Third World Gay Caucus. The
term "third world gay" extends back at least as far as the late
1960s. One of the earliest uses of the term seems to have
been by the group Third World Gay Revolution, which developed as a caucus of New York's Gay Liberation Front.
For them, the term indicated a political identification of
racial solidarity that was also a commitment to revolutionary socialist and anti-colonial struggle throughout the world
(Third World Gay Revolution 1971). Their explicitly third-
world alignment also reflected back on the anti-colonial and
transnational political commitments that originally infused
GLF, which took its name in solidarity with the National
Liberation Front of South Vietnam (Kissack 1995, 113–16).
As its late-1960s origins receded into the distance, "third
world gay" did not always retain its original meaning and
political connotations. Sometimes it was used more neu- Pol
trally to describe a gay man or lesbian of color, though at
other times it continued to circulate as a politicized identification, as during the National Third World Lesbian and
Gay Conference, which coincided with the first national gay

and lesbian march on Washington in October 1979.[39] When the term "third world gay" appears in *Word Is Out*, it is never explicitly linked to an anti-colonial or transnational political framework, and yet its very appearance points to spaces beyond and before the film's alignment with a gay liberal agenda.

Anti-colonial

Transnational

Just as gender parity in the collective was seen as a means to achieve gender parity in the final film, the filmmakers' methods for bringing diversity to the project along other axes of difference, such as race, age, political conviction, and class, were often very straightforward. At a March 1976 screening of a rough cut of the film—which at that time included only the first eight people interviewed on celluloid, all of whom read as white—Nancy Adair explained to the audience what was on the agenda: "Andrew will be traveling back East to look for a black man, Rob will look for young men, and I will be going South to find a lesbian feminist" (1978, 287). Although there were exceptions to this identity match game, the structuring premise was that people spoke

39. See, for instance, the reports and speeches from the conference collected in *Gay Insurgent* 6 (1980): 11–21. I am grateful to everyone who responded, especially Marc Stein and Daniel Tsang, to my inquiry on the Qstudy listserv about shifts in the political uses and connotations of "third world gay" across the 1970s. José Esteban Muñoz discusses Third World Gay Revolution's manifesto, in contradistinction to "the anemic political agenda that dominates contemporary LGBT politics in North America today," in his book *Cruising Utopia* (2008, 19).

best to individuals like themselves, even as the film itself sought to encourage identifications across difference.

The statements made by lesbians and gay men of color in *Word Is Out* seldom indicate alternatives to or complications of normative framings of gay and lesbian experience. In most cases, the statements and their speakers are readily in- *[cut content]* corporated into the film's composite portrait. The politics of race in and around *Word Is Out* become more complex when one moves beyond the surface of the final film and examines the celluloid rushes and video pre-interviews. Although one cannot know for certain why any given content, pertaining to race or any other subject matter, did or did not make it into the final film, a comparison of the final film with the interviews that preceded it is revealing. It seems that not every statement made by interviewees of color could fit neatly into the film's portrait of a universal gay liberal subject, and those statements that were most resistant seem to have been the ones that articulate a third world gay identification and analysis (see also "V Is for Video").

Chiu first appears in Part Two of the film, seated at a small table in the living room of a sunlit apartment. He recounts an innocent tale of an early gay experience and reflects on his experience broadly as a Chinese-American gay man. To- *[Chinaman vs. fag ↓]* ward the very end of the film he says, "You go through a lot of hurt when somebody calls you a 'Chinaman.' And so you're in one sense more able to deal with someone call- ing you a 'fag.' And you can spring back more easily and

[Assumption vs. truth]

FIGURE 25. Dennis Chiu in the final minutes of *Word is Out*: "You go through a lot of hurt when someone calls you a Chinaman ..." DVD still.

say, 'I'm a person. I am me.'" The statement presents Chiu's experiences overcoming racism as something that lends him strength in his efforts to overcome homophobia and in his quest to be recognized as a full person. Throughout the film, Chiu speaks slowly and thoughtfully. At times he hesitates, as if he is searching for the right words to convey his meaning. By my impression, he seems a bit unsure of himself. He lacks the easy, confident speech of Pat Bond, Sally Gearhart, and Rick Stokes.

Rob Epstein conducted the celluloid interview with Chiu,

the transcript of which appears in the book that accompanies the film. Throughout most of the interview Epstein's questions do not engage with issues of race and ethnicity, though Chiu's answers often do. At the end of the interview Epstein asks about the experience of "gay Asians" directly, but the questions are non-specific and open-ended (N. Adair and C. Adair 1978, 188–90). By contrast, in Andrew Brown's video pre-interview with Chiu, the conversation returns again and again to the topic of racism within what Chiu calls the "quote unquote gay community," a topic absent from the final film. In this interview, Chiu is as critical of racial injustice among gay people as he is of gay identity and culture as a whole. Although he is upset that Asian-American gay men are not included in many white gay spaces and subcultures because of racism, he is as upset, perhaps more so, that Asian-American gay men often internalize the racist and sexist values of white gay male culture. He speaks at one point of the need to "drive out those white demons in a lot of Chinese people's minds." Brown asks Chiu if he thinks there are gay people in China, and Chiu explodes at the question. He articulates a strong critique of the ways white Western concerns about sexual repression have been used to undermine the Cultural Revolution. He argues that Western efforts to push "a sexual trip" onto China divert energy and attention away from the real issue: the exploitative role of Western interests there.

Throughout the video pre-interview, Chiu is smart, passionate, and confident. It is impossible to know why he

[margin annotation: Exclusion of Asian-Americans]

seems so markedly different on video than he does in the final film. Perhaps it is because he is speaking to another gay man of color. Perhaps it is because he is discussing topics that interest and inspire him more than those of the later interview. Perhaps it is because he knows that the video pre-interview will not be a permanent and public record in the same way that the film interview will be. Or perhaps it is because by the time of the film interview his own politics have become more in sync with the film's liberal-human-ist framing.[40] Whatever the explanation, the person in the video pre-interview, with his impassioned critique of white, Western racism and imperialism, seems unassimilable to the argument and ideology of the final film.

western racism not a focus

---

40. I asked Dennis Chiu about the trajectory of his statements from the video pre-interview to the final film in an email exchange in late April 2011. He does not recall the video interview very well, but he made it clear that he has moved some distance from his younger self, and that he finds the full celluloid conversation, as presented in the accompanying book to the film, to be very dated: "It stems from the need to map out some ideological territory that in retrospect is highly risible and contrived, to say the least." He continues to feel ambivalent about gay identification and gay male culture.

U IS FOR USA

In his book *Gay Rights and Moral Panic: The Origins of America's Debate on Homosexuality*, Fred Fejes argues that the late-1970s series of local but nationally mediated gay-rights contestations (in Miami, St. Paul, Wichita, Eugene, Seattle, and the state of California) fostered a new national identity among gay men and lesbians in the US. "Emerging during these months was what political scholar Benedict Anderson described as 'an imagined community,' a community defined not by physical space and boundaries or the actual physical contact among its members but by the mental image of affinity—'the image of communion'—that each held in their minds" (2008, 215).

Because *Word Is Out* privileges domestic spaces, it is difficult to know where geographically most of its scenes unfold. In order to expand on the film's foundations in the San Francisco Bay Area, the filmmakers conducted interviews in Massachusetts, New Mexico, New York, North Carolina, Pennsylvania, and Washington, DC, though viewers can hardly be faulted for imagining that it ranges even farther, throughout the US and perhaps into English-speaking Canada. The film's ambiguity as to the "physical space and boundaries" of the community it imagines contributed to its impressive circulation abroad, where it could be received as universal in theme rather than a report on US-specific experiences.

[handwritten marginalia: Seemingly geographically universal]

This is not to say that the film's national origins ever disappeared or became immaterial. The film traveled to Cuba in 1983, as part of *La otra cara* (The Other Face), a showcase of recent leftist North American independent cinema. There, the film became the center of a quiet controversy when authorities from the national film institute failed to translate its subtitles along with an essay about gay aesthetics written by co-programmer B. Ruby Rich. Although the wrongs were set right the next day, it is clear that in this context everyone understood *Word Is Out* as a US cinematic production that sought to infiltrate the country with a representation of homosexuality oppositional to the party line.[41]

Back in the states, two documentaries presented alternate visions of the newly imagined national community of gay men and lesbians. Arthur Bressan's *Gay USA* (1978) draws on the public forum of the Gay Pride parade to construct a counter-referendum to the one orchestrated by Anita Bryant in Dade County. In the few weeks between Bryant's June 7, 1977, "Orange Tuesday" victory and the Pride marches tak-

---

41. I thank B. Ruby Rich for filling me in on the history of *Word Is Out* in Cuba. A full account of the story will be included in her forthcoming book *New Queer Cinema: The Complete Collection*, due out in 2012. *Word Is Out* traveled throughout Latin America in 1985 as part of a touring version of the *La otra cara* program. The Peter Adair Papers contain materials pertaining to the tour and to the film's other travels abroad, including a number of prestigious festival screenings and theatrical engagements in Western Europe (box 33, folders 2, 3, and 5).

ing place later that month, Bressan coordinated film crews to shoot footage of five parades across the nation: Chicago, Los Angeles, New York, San Diego, and San Francisco (though, as in *Word Is Out*, San Francisco predominates). The film is comprised mainly of on-the-street interviews, with both gays and straights, both marchers and onlookers, and, among this last, both friendly and hostile witnesses. The film revels in the carnivalesque nature of the parades and their function *Pride* as sites of ideological contestation. By contrasting the pa- *parades* rades to the totalitarian spectacle of Nazi Germany's 1934 Nuremburg Rally, represented through intercut footage of Leni Riefenstahl's *Triumph des Willens* (*Triumph of the Will*, 1935), Bressan's film manages to make the most *outré* elements of the US parades into "positive images" of how the public sphere is supposed to function in a healthy and non-oppressive democratic society.

Rosa von Praunheim's *Army of Lovers, or Revolt of the Perverts* (1979) also formulates a vision of "gay USA." Praunheim originally intended his film to be a history of US gay and lesbian politics throughout the decade, under the working title "From Stonewall to Anita" (Kelly 1979, 115). He was especially interested in how Bryant's campaign seemed to have reenergized gay activism after a mid-1970s lull. But by the time his film appeared in 1979, it had also become an exposé and plea for marginalized lifestyles that were under assault from a consolidating, anxious, and boundary-policing gay liberalism. Particularly in the second half, the film becomes an idiosyncratic and sensationalist ethnographic account of US gay male life. Praunheim leads the viewer on a whirlwind tour of the late-1970s sexual fringe: street cruising, pornography, sex clubs, hustling, a gay Nazi (what I meant by "idiosyncratic and sensationalist"), and man-boy love. Unlike the collaborative design of both *Word Is Out* and *Gay USA*, *Army of Lovers* is defiantly <u>auteurist</u>.

Filmmaker control

Nevertheless, the film stages some of the confrontations across difference that are missing from *Word Is Out*. For instance, Praunheim interviews a lesbian feminist who is outraged about gay male misogyny and a sexualized performance by Grace Jones at the 1978 Christopher Street Liberation Day parade in New York. Praunheim is fairly passive during the interview, for the most part simply listening as the woman states her position. His consciousness-raising occurs on the film's voiceover track after the interview is over, as we see him head to the baths and then to Central Park to decompress. "I have never liked lesbians. I feel threatened by their strength and demands and self-awareness. I feel their criticism and hostility for men. Now I have learned that lesbians have to struggle hard against a society in which they are doubly repressed, as women and as lesbians. But does this knowledge change me?" This is hardly a breakthrough in the history of lesbian and gay male relating; certainly, what went on behind the scenes of *Word Is Out* built more bridges. However, because of Praunheim's persistence in acknowledging and recording conflicts within

Lesbian Feminists ↔ gay male misogynists

FIGURE 26. A rare instance in the 1970s of gay men and lesbians appearing together onscreen and discussing their differences: Rosa von Praunheim interviews a lesbian feminist who is upset about gay male misogyny in *Army of Lovers, or Revolt of the Perverts* (1979). DVD still. Courtesy of Rosa von Praunheim.

gay and lesbian politics, as well as his penchant for uncovering marginalized subjects and "negative images," his film is an invaluable record of the complexity and range of 1970s gay culture. Perhaps its most valuable footage is of a meeting of the Boston/Boise Committee, the group that organized to defend the men accused in the 1977 Revere sex ring scandal in Massachusetts, and out of which the North-American Man-Boy Love Association (NAMBLA) would soon form.

With content like this, *Army of Lovers* provides a more wide-ranging survey of mid- to late-1970s US gay attitudes and politics than even the vast collection of video pre-interviews created for *Word Is Out*.

Although it became newly possible in the late 1970s to imagine a gay community that was coextensive with the US, the definition of this new gay nation was still up for grabs. Who got to be a citizen and where was political action to take place: in the privacy of the home, at the heart of the crowd marching down main street, or in the margins of the sexual fringe? Although a liberal framing of responsible gay and lesbian citizenship was clearly ascendant, positions further to the Left and anti-gay forces to the Right both challenged gay liberalism's fragile claims to legitimacy and representation by moving obscene elements back onto the screen. *Gay USA* and *Army of Lovers* had little exposure in the US beyond urban gay audiences. By contrast, through its public television broadcast, *Word Is Out* established a direct line of communication from the homes of its interview subjects to the homes of its viewers, virtually cutting out altogether the unruly sites of queer public culture that are on view in the other two films.

[handwritten marginal note:] Sphere / spheres: / - Public / - Pseudo / - Private / - (Technical)

[handwritten note:] Why 's a private topic in the public sphere?

[handwritten note:] How does the technical sphere of the law play a role?

V IS FOR VIDEO

> I don't know, Veronica. I would like to speak very directly
> and precisely to what you're asking, but I can't.
> —Audre Lorde, in her video pre-interview for the film

The video pre-interviews for *Word Is Out* are strikingly different from the final film. With their perfunctory, low-resolution, black-and-white imagery, they pale in comparison to the translucent color and thoughtful mise-en-scène of the celluloid footage. Some of the video pre-interviews wander from topic to topic, but others are surprisingly focused, at least from the interviewer's end of things. In order to produce an effective screen test, the filmmakers had a set of questions that needed to be asked and answered within the length of the available tape. In the early days of video, tape was cheap, but it was not yet as cheap as we now think of it in comparison to film. The filmmakers used donated, recycled videotape and preserved space on the thirty-minute reels whenever possible, often stopping the recorder at pauses in the interviews and when they asked their questions. As such, one of the most jarring things about the video pre-interviews is the editing: it is always in-camera and it is never smooth. The cuts indicate the awkwardness of the exchange between interviewer and interviewee in a way that the carefully composed edit of the final film does not.[42]

Although Betty Powell is the only black lesbian to appear in *Word Is Out*, there were others interviewed on video, among them Pat Parker (1944–1989) and Audre Lorde (1934–1992), two prominent poets and cultural activists of the period. Veronica Selver conducted the video pre-interview with Lorde. By my viewing of the tape, Selver's abstractly personal questions seem jarringly at odds with the charged responses of the self-proclaimed "warrior poet." Although some disconnect between question and answer is to be expected in an exploratory interview, here it approaches the absurd. When Selver says to Lorde, "Tell me about your coming out," Lorde responds by querying the scope and meaning of the question:

coming out
as what
and how

> Um, so when you speak of coming out, do you mean
> coming out as a black woman who is determined to
> make her own way? Do you mean coming out as a
> poet who knows that she must write or die? Do you
> mean coming out as a woman who loves women and
> feels she has a right to? Coming out as a woman who
> loves women and who also wants to have children?

42. The Mariposa Film Group conducted over 140 video pre-interviews on half-inch open-reel videotape. In 1991, these reels were transferred to three-quarter-inch masters and VHS viewing copies, both of which are housed at the San Francisco Public Library.

Coming out, I don't know. I have been at war as long as I can remember. It has made me tough, but it has also made me weary. Do I ... Am I speaking to what you're asking me?

On video, Selver does not answer. She mumbles "um, just a minute" and there is a break in the tape. She likely turned the camera off as she figured out her next question. Perhaps she responded to Lorde then and a rich conversation ensued about different definitions of coming out. However, nothing on the video after the break indicates that Lorde's statement has affected the course of the interview, despite the challenge she has just posed to the structuring premise of the film project. Selver's next two questions are about Lorde's experiences at college and her relationship with her two children.

During a lengthy monologue, which seems to have taken off from Selver's request that she talk about her "love for women" (though there are again intervening skips in the tape), Lorde lists specific examples of prejudice and lived injustice, e.g., racial slurs hurled at her children as they walk down the street, and a prominent lesbian feminist saying of lesbian mothers that "if they were lesbians they wouldn't be mothers." She then explores the relationship between self-hatred and hatred of others:

LORDE: I'm speaking about the urge in each one of

us to oppress anyone who is different. And it is that urge that I fight against more than any other.

SELVER: Hm-mm.

LORDE: The urge to destroy that indestructible part of yourself that you don't want to accept. Hey, the energy that it takes doing that, you know, we could use to clean up the streams.

SELVER: Hm-mm.

LORDE: Are you hearing what I'm saying? Ay, Veronica. Yoo hoo!

With Lorde's "Yoo hoo!", the video camera suddenly reveals itself to be a wall between interviewer and interviewee, an awkward barrier to communication that Lorde must shout across to be heard. The way media technology impedes the back-and-forth responsiveness of the interview at this moment is precisely what the filmmakers worked so hard to prevent from happening, or at least to prevent from seeming like it was happening, during the film interviews (see "I Is for Interview").

I asked Selver about her interview with Lorde in an email exchange toward the end of my preparation of this book.[43]

---

43. Selver's response, which I quote and paraphrase here, is from April 6, 2011.

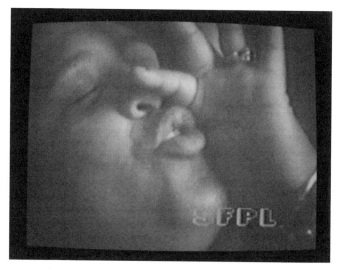

FIGURE 27. "Yoo hoo! Veronica, can you hear me?" Audre Lorde during her video pre-interview for *Word Is Out*. VHS screenshot. Courtesy of the San Francisco Public Library and the Mariposa Film Group.

She countered my impression that she and Lorde were not communicating. She recalls instead that the exchange had a teasing, "cat and mouse playfulness," in which the older, wiser Lorde was the City Cat and young Selver the Country Mouse. It is certainly true that there is a good-natured, even flirtatious quality to Lorde's conduct. Selver tried to recall why the filmmakers did not select Lorde for the film. She seems to remember that Lorde overwhelmed the group when they watched the tape and that they worried she might dominate the film. Rob Epstein (whom Selver in turn asked about the matter) wonders if Lorde was already too much of a star to fit comfortably within the film, though he also says that when the filmmakers heard her response to the query about coming out, they probably feared she would complicate the film with too many issues.

When Betty Powell asks at the beginning of *Word Is Out* if the filmmakers are aware that black lesbians "come in all shapes and colors and directions to our lives" and if they are capturing that in the film, one gets the impression that her vision of diversity is compatible with the film's: in other words, that the main problem is underrepresentation, and that if there were more individual interviews with black lesbians distributed across the film, then the problem would be solved. By contrast, Lorde's approach to difference seems structurally incompatible with the liberal vision of a mosaic of diversity. In her writings and speeches, Lorde asked her audience to engage directly and creatively with difference. "Difference must be not merely tolerated, but seen as a fund of necessary polarities between which our creativity can spark like a dialectic. Only then does the necessity for interdependency become unthreatening" (1979, 111). Lorde's dialectical approach demands a coming together of individuals to confront the things that keep them apart. Had she made the leap from video to film, she would have been shouting across the camera and pushing against the edges of the frame to make contact.

W IS FOR WORD

> We have been made invisible because the word might get
> out that women can love each other. We have been made
> invisible because the word might get out that men can love
> each other.
> —Sally Gearhart speaking at 1977 Gay Freedom Day
> parade in San Francisco

It is strange that it took so long for a major talking-head
documentary about lesbians and gay men to appear. Most
social movements that were active in the 1970s turned to the
interview format early on as a way to air and legitimize the
voices of marginalized people, for instance people of color
and members of the working class. The format was a staple
of women's movement filmmaking from the very beginning of the decade, in such films as *Growing Up Female* (Julia Reichert and James Klein, 1971) and *The Woman's Film*
(San Francisco Newsreel, 1971), largely because the format
synced up so well with the practice of consciousness rais-
ing: moving around the circle and hearing ordinary women
recount their life experiences in the new light of feminism
(Erens 1988, Lesage 1984). However, before a gay and lesbian interview film could arrive on the scene, a major shift
had to occur in the paradigms of coming out and gay "visibility," to the point where being openly gay was no longer

of necessity a visual phenomenon and could instead be expressed more purely in the realm of talk, talk, talk.

Like many interview documentaries, *Word Is Out* was edited more by speech than by image. Transcripts of the interviews were typed up on color-coded pieces of paper, a different color for each person in the film. The words were then cut up into thematic segments, which the filmmakers selected from and arranged on a large bulletin board. In this way they were able to quickly and easily swap out material and reorder sequences.[44] In her account of the filmmaking process, Nancy Adair refers to the vérité interludes as "visual sequences," as if the main bulk of the film were not visual. The filmmakers shot quite a bit of vérité material, but in the end they decided that they needed to return to "the original form" of the film: "predominantly talking heads with occasional music and visual breaks" (N. Adair 1978, 304). The scarcity of vérité material means that the standard interview-documentary tactic of using archival footage and still photography to support claims made on the audio track is kept to a minimum. As an especially bare talking-head documentary, *Word Is Out* arguably derives little of its truth-value from the visual and indexical guarantees of celluloid. It is not clear what there is onscreen to make the filmed testimonies

44. An image and description of the editing board is provided in N. Adair (1978, 303). In the Adair Papers I also came across a beautiful Polaroid image, apparently taken at twilight, of multicolored pieces of paper arranged in a grid-like pattern beneath a large bay window.

any more "real" than the printed interview transcripts in the companion book. *Word Is Out* presents coming out, and being out, as primarily about speech and feeling rather than image or action.

In speech act theory, the constative utterance, which is used to describe something or state a fact, is contrasted to the performative utterance, which performs an action through speech. Classic examples of the performative utterance are "I do" (in a wedding ceremony), "I apologize," and "I promise." The statement is the action, and through the act of making the statement a change of state occurs in the speaker (Austin 1976). Saying "I am gay" is a performative speech act to the extent that it is the statement that constitutes the act of coming out: by saying the words one is presumably transformed into an openly gay person. But what exactly does this mean? What change of state is meant to have occurred in the subject through the statement, and how does one know that it actually took place? In his lectures on performative speech acts, J.L. Austin spends a lot of time trying to figure out how to determine if a given performative utterance is felicitous, that is, whether it successfully carries out the action it is meant to perform (ibid., 12–52). He talks about the conventions that must be in place; the appropriateness of the circumstances; the correctness of procedure; and then, what is far more difficult to determine, whether the speaker truly means what she says and whether her subsequent conduct provides evidence that the change of state has in fact occurred (ibid., 14–15). But how and when is a coming-out statement felicitous?

This question is obviously extraordinarily unethical when one imagines it being posed to any given "out" gay person. It stirs up images of dogmatic groups that prescribe and then scrutinize the behavior and appearance of their members in order to monitor the depth of their commitment to the cause (and there were certainly a few lesbian-separatist and gay-radical groups in the 1970s that did just that). But putting aside the ethical difficulty of the question, on a more broadly historical level it remains a useful one. In the late 1970s, as the site where gayness happens moved from the spheres of vision and action into those of speech and soul, it became more difficult to assess the felicity of the coming-out statement, at least in relation to any real-world referent. The statement was no longer definitionally bound up with sexual, bodily, political, or sartorial transgression, either at the time of its utterance or as a necessary consequence from it down the line. Instead, as *Word Is Out* demonstrates perhaps more than any other cultural work of gay liberalism, the coming-out statement became an action that would ideally transform the subject through speech alone, ushering in a new era of the person who, for better and for worse, can calmly assert "I am gay" and then sit there complacently, looking and acting no differently but feeling wonderful.

X IS FOR XXX

In 1977, as the makers of *Word Is Out* were shooting their final footage and racing to finish post-production, Rosa von Praunheim was across town using celluloid to make a very different argument about the truth of homosexuality. The San Francisco Art Institute had invited the West German filmmaker to teach a filmmaking course. In a short sequence of his film *Army of Lovers, or Revolt of the Perverts* (1979), we see footage of one of his lessons as he explains his teaching philosophy in voiceover:

> I taught a production class, and for the film my students made I chose the theme of homosexuality. I presented myself and my private life as a study. In one of the first classes, I asked my students to film me as I showed them exactly what gay sex is. As a partner, I invited Glen, a model I had seen in a porno movie. I think it's very important to make private life public. Prejudice comes from ignorance, from rumor, from anxiety before the unknown. If we want people's attitudes towards sex to change, we have to demystify it and face the simple truth about sex courageously. The performance left my students speechless but I enjoyed it very much.

Make private public.

FIGURE 28. Meanwhile, elsewhere in San Francisco ... : Rosa von Praunheim teaches his students a different truth about homosexuality. DVD still from *Army of Lovers, or Revolt of the Perverts* (1979). Courtesy of Rosa von Praunheim.

The image track presents Rosa and Glen naked in the middle of the classroom. They take turns fellating each other under the hot studio lights, while young art students circle around and absorb the spectacle. The students are clad in underwear and lingerie; some of them have cameras, and some do not. After this, for another minute, the film presents a sustained shot of Praunheim performing oral sex in medium close-up, as the film's other male voiceover (a disembodied, American-accented voice of authority) describes San Francisco as "the world's gayest city," but also a "sunshine ghetto [that] is not representative of the general attitude toward gays in America."

Obviously, Praunheim's understanding of the essence of gay private life and his notion of the best way to change straight people's minds about homosexuality differed significantly from the ideas of the Mariposa Film Group. By one perspective, Praunheim wallows in the definition of homosexuality that liberal, humanist approaches sought to break free of: the reduction of gay personhood to sexual desires and practices. By another perspective, his sexual-libertarian effort to shed affirming light on stigmatized sexual practices, as well as his gay-liberationist effort to use those practices as leverage against heteronormativity, aligns him with an international roster of filmmakers in the 1970s who sought to liberate gay people by liberating gay sex. At the end of Christopher Larkin's *A Very Natural Thing* (1974), the two male protagonists frolic together naked on an empty beach. Similarly wide-open spaces underpin the erotic visions of Derek Jarman and Paul Humfress's *Sebastiane* (1976), Philippe Vallois' *Johan* (1976), many of Barbara Hammer's experimental shorts, and numerous other films of the era, including countless more straightforwardly pornographic titles. Films of all persuasions tended to set scenes of "out" gay life in lush but oddly barren landscapes. (Indeed, many of the films just listed unfold in what appear to be the same sunlit, bird-chirpy meadows in which Linda Marco and David Gillon sit for their interviews and Harry Hay and John Burnside stroll together hand in hand.) Praunheim's film stands apart from the pack not because two gay men have sex onscreen or in "public"—that happened in hundreds of films—but because there are so many other people in the frame, presumably many of them straight, who are made to watch.

Moving in the other direction, filmmakers Nancy Adair, Rob Epstein, Lucy Massie Phenix, and Veronica Selver have all stated, either in print or during my interviews with them, that one of the main goals of *Word Is Out* was to demonstrate that gay relationships were not just about sex.[45] Many of them point to Gillon's testimony at the end of Part Two, when he tells of his sex-free relationship with another man, as an especially significant and emotionally powerful moment in the film. Epstein, who was tasked with recruiting younger gay men for the film, was instrumental in bringing Gillon on board and shaping the interview. It is Epstein's voice that is heard off camera, interjecting an affirmative "That's beautiful!" at the end of Gillon's tale. In her account

Not just sex

45. I interviewed Massie Phenix and Selver together on March 20, 2009, and Rob Epstein on June 8, 2009. Peter Adair seems to have been the Mariposan who was most ambivalent about the ideological implications of the film's argument for coupling and romantic love: "I think it's funny that in some ways the film makes implications that I don't feel real comfortable making, and that is that romantic love is an answer. An answer to anything" (Mariposa Film Group 1977, 24). In the same interview Adair expresses concern about the film's sidelining of gay male sex and sexuality (ibid., 23).

FIGURE 29. A sex-free tale of true love: David Gillon in the daisy patch. DVD still.

of the film's making, Nancy Adair expressed a similar desire behind the decision to conduct a celluloid interview with Cynthia Gair and her roommate/business partner Helaine Harris (though the footage with Harris did not make it into the final film). "We wanted to point out in the film that gay people have strong friendships with each other, which do not necessarily involve sex" (N. Adair 1978, 300).

Some of the letters that the filmmakers received from viewers testify to the value of this strategy. The writers, including some who say they have never had sex, express gratitude for the film's presentation of lesbians and gay men who talk about their lives without reducing everything to the sexual act. However, at the same time that *Word Is Out* presents an affirming reflection for these viewers, one that they had trouble finding among other cinematic portrayals of lesbians and gay men during the decade, the film also falsely suggests a generational movement beyond carnality, toward post-sexual forms and definitions of gay life.

False
Movement
of definition
of gay life

Y IS FOR YOUTH

As the theatrical run of *Word Is Out* was winding down, the filmmakers made a forty-five-minute version of the film intended for non-theatrical exhibition, particularly in classrooms.[46] The short, educational version marked a late return of the project to Peter Adair's original design: a media tool intended to reach closeted gay youth in high schools, colleges, and community groups. It features "Conversations with 16 gay men and women"—excising ten or so interview subjects—and it subtly but significantly reorders the footage.

The educational version seems less concerned than the final film with reflexivity and with presenting a representative cross-section of gays and lesbians in the US. It does not begin with a charmingly flub-filled opening sequence, nor is there the mirrored footage with Roger Harkenrider to drive home the filmmakers' presence and involvement. Harkenrider, the film's spokesperson for "faggotry," is gone, as is Mark Pinney, the film's token conservative. Betty Powell remains, but she never asks a direct question about the film's presentation of black lesbians. As far as racial representation goes, Nadine Armijo, Rosa Montoya, and Donald Hackett

---

46. A 16mm print of this version is housed in the Adair Papers, box 57. Documentation in the archive indicates that Rob Epstein produced the short version, working on it from October 1979 to January 1980 (box 33, folder 20).

are also missing. Perhaps the most notable absence is cultural feminism, which is felt very strongly in the full film. The
educational cut has no Elsa Gidlow, no Ann Samsell, and no
Cynthia Gair, nor is there any music from Trish Nugent.
(The gay male group Buena Vista still performs.) Whitey
Fladden remains, but she has no empowering scene in the
woods with a chainsaw. Sally Gearhart is still here, but no
one asks her about separatism.

As for what doesn't change: most of the rich content of
Part One is still here. George Mendenhall, Pat Bond, Rick
Stokes, Pam Jackson, and Rusty Millington continue to be
strong onscreen presences, as does Tede Matthews who still
debunks myths of gender in Part Two.[47] What feels newest
to the educational cut is the more clearly shaped rhetorical
and narrative emphasis on coming out, as well as the stronger presence of David Gillon. With both Gair and Nick
Dorsky absent, Gillon now carries the end of Part Two on
his own. Interestingly, he also now carries the end of Part
Three and thus the film itself. In the film's final moments,
Gillon tells the suspenseful story of coming out to his father,
with a cut to the Freedom Day parade montage right after
he says, "He didn't blink." Rather than leave its youth audience stranded in the limbo of an ill-defined, post-out "From

[handwritten marginal note: focus on coming out]

---

47. The educational version does not present title cards that
explicitly break the film into parts, but musical interludes and
fades to black function to convey what remains a strong three-part
structure.

FIGURE 30. The more things change ... : Terry Miller and Dan Savage use the talking-head format to reach out to a new generation of gay youth. Video screenshot. Courtesy of the It Gets Better Project.

Now On," the educational version presents coming out to one's family as the culminating step of the journey to freedom and self-acceptance.

Word Is Out has striking similarities to the *It Gets Better* project, which is also a talking-head media project that is geared toward queer youth, but that presents and consolidates a national portrait of queer adults. The project was created by syndicated sex-columnist Dan Savage along with his partner Terry Miller in the wake of a series of gay teen suicides in late 2010. It consists of an ever-growing number of videos on YouTube as well as on the project's web site, *itgetsbetter.org*. As with *Word Is Out*, the majority of the *It Gets Better* videos present individuals and couples in domestic settings who recount simple narratives of their lives in direct address to the camera.[48] As in *Word Is Out*, many of the videos begin with specific and often visceral stories of trauma in "the early years," but then get hazier as they move into the present. Both projects savvily use media (public television in the late 1970s, the Internet today) to sneak their affirming messages past phobic institutional watchdogs and cultural gatekeepers in order to reach queer youth directly. Both projects were also designed to target young people who do not have access to the sites of queer activism and support that are often clustered in cities.

Perhaps the strangest thing about *It Gets Better* is how similar the project is to *Word Is Out* despite today's vastly changed mediascape. We are a far cry from the late 1970s, when it was still possible to claim that no gay-produced, gay-positive media was reaching the hinterlands. Nevertheless, the *It Gets Better* project's structuring premise is that queer youth today have trouble finding affirming media

48. The first video of the project, featuring Miller and Savage, was shot at a bar with a professional microphone clearly visible in frame. A filmmaker friend of theirs made the video, interviewing them and then editing the footage (Savage 2011, 4–5). Most of the videos contributed to the project are much more simply and directly made, using webcams and without any editing.

representations, even in the age of Google (which at the time of this writing in 2011 just became a supporter of the project through a major television ad campaign). Ironically, the project is able to promote the impression that it is the lone queer-positive voice in the homo- and transphobic wilderness precisely because it is supported and endorsed by a huge network of mainstream media sites and prominent US institutions, from Ellen to *Glee*, from Lady Gaga to the White House.

The *It Gets Better* project is a culmination of historical developments in US gay cultural activism that were only beginning to take shape and gain ground in the late 1970s, when *Word Is Out* succeeded in its Herculean efforts to gain access to homes and schools where closeted gay youth could encounter its positive message. The youth orientation of the projects is key to understanding both their affective power and their political moderation. They present a goal that is impossible to refuse or criticize—what queer person does not want to prevent queer youth from hating and harming themselves?—and in doing so they demand, justify, and naturalize the reduction of queer politics to a lowest-common-denominator agenda and vision. This in turn ends up legitimizing normative positions on adjacent issues. The *It Gets Better* project, for instance, while ostensibly having nothing to do with the issue of gay marriage, clearly valorizes it as one of the primary features of "better" LGBT adulthood. For these reasons, neither project should be understood simply as strategic liberalism or as a simplification of queer politics in order to get one's message out to those who need it most. Both *Word Is Out* and *It Gets Better* present queer youth with a very limited set of ways to understand themselves and their possible futures. And because of the centripetal pull of the two projects, they also determine and delimit the self-understandings and political imaginations of queer adults: indeed, the diversity of gay activists who have contributed videos to the *It Gets Better* project is perhaps even broader than the mix of movement luminaries who agreed to be pre-interviewed for *Word Is Out*.[49]

Youth and their futures

49. Among the gay cultural and political activists who gave pre-interviews for *Word Is Out* are Tom Ammiano, Virginia Apuzzo, Blackberri, Charlotte Bunch, Bertha Harris, Helaine Harris, Dolores Klaich, Audre Lorde, Carole Migden, Pat Norman, Pat Parker, Howard Wallace, Hank Wilson, and Claude Wynne. This is by no means an exhaustive list. The San Francisco Public Library's online guide to the Peter Adair Papers includes a full list of the video pre-interview subjects: sfpl.org/pdf/main/glc/GLC70_Peter_Adair_Papers.pdf

Z IS FOR ZOOM

If one watches *Word Is Out* with the knowledge that the camera operator is also asking the questions and that all but one of the interview subjects (Mark Pinney) was originally pre-interviewed on video, one has a keen sense of the filmmakers lying in wait with their zoom lens. They incite and then pounce on the moments in the subjects' testimonies that have been preselected as revelatory: the sustained close-up on Pat Bond after Nancy Adair has spurred her to drop the mask of humor; or the intercut extreme close-ups of Whitey Fladden and Rick Stokes—their chins and the tops of their heads cropped out of the frame—as they recount their experiences with psychiatric "cures." The film's use of the zoom lens is similar to its deployment in the 1970s narrative films of Robert Altman, where it is also a main tool of the cameraperson's half-improvisational response to the actors' half-improvisational performances. Throughout *Word Is Out*, the various zoom-ins are the film's most ostentatious flourishes of cinematography, eruptions of clear emotional manipulation within a talking-head structure that otherwise seldom calls attention to itself.

With its use of the zoom, *Word Is Out* also formalizes political and ontological shifts in gay and lesbian life at the end of the 1970s. As it zooms in, the film inscribes homosexuality as deep subjectivity, a truth at the level of the soul. The

FIGURE 31. Zooming in on the essential truths of gay and lesbian experience: Whitey Fladden talks in extreme close-up about having been institutionalized because of her homosexuality. DVD still.

formal technique supports the film's project of displacing vision to voice. As one moves in on each speaker's face in privileged, revelatory moments, the visuality of gay and lesbian life and its larger historical and political context move to the edges of the screen: the bodily and sartorial differences of Tede Mathews and Rusty Millington; the sex acts that for George Mendenhall and Rick Stokes are definitional of gay life; and the various political commitments of Sally Gearhart, Harry Hay, and Betty Powell. Everything clears the frame in order to make room for the leveling, universalizing,

Pushes away politics + political historical frames

and magnetic presence of the face in close-up. *Word Is Out* demonstrates that the gay liberal politics of visibility has always been about rendering gays and lesbians, in one sense, functionally invisible—which is to say, visually undifferentiated from everyone else.

Human like everyone

In part to work against this, I have tried in this book to zoom out, pulling back from *Word Is Out* and its onscreen subjects in order to resituate them within their historical context. I have brought into the picture many details from the film's long and complex history of production, as well as biographical information about some of its key participants. I have also contrasted the film with other works of 1970s gay and lesbian activist filmmaking that are not in mainstream circulation and are therefore less frequently remembered. In doing all this I hope I have laid bare the formal, historical, and political specificity of a film that, as I pointed out in my introduction, often passes as formless, timeless, and apolitical. At the same time, in pulling out for this wider shot, I hope that I have not become so critically distant that I have failed to appreciate the power of seeing the face in close-up, or the way that simply taking the time to listen to the story of another person's life can enable identifications and affinities that trespass the boundaries of one's own politics and experience.

As I write this, I am thirty-three years old, the age that Peter Adair was in 1976 when he shot much of the celluloid footage for *Word Is Out*. The other filmmakers were in their mid-thirties on down. Rob Epstein, the youngest of the bunch, was only twenty-one. This is of course humbling, as my book can hardly measure up to the accomplishment of the film. The parallel helps me appreciate the filmmakers' own efforts and successes in forging connections across queer generations. If I have been critical in these pages of their presentation of the twentysomethings of Part Two, I have great respect for the openness to cross-generational and cross-experiential conversation that shaped the film project as a whole, and which for me is best evinced by the magical moments with the older subjects of Part One.

Cross-generational by young filmmakers

As I think about my own efforts to connect to the queer past and to the experience of older queer people in the present, I realize that in our current world, which seems so removed from the revolutionary potentials of the 1960s and 1970s, I hunger for more than the face in radiant close-up, and for more than hagiographic stories of gay and lesbian pioneers. I need the dirt and the conflict. I need to hear how the queer people who came before me have struggled with the most difficult issues of queer history, community, and politics. I am very grateful that the Mariposa Film Group made *Word Is Out* and for the work they did to change hearts and minds in the late 1970s, but I am as grateful that they preserved the rich and often turbulent exchanges leading up to and surrounding the project. The archive has opened up my experience of the film in a myriad of unexpected ways, in part by enabling me to see beyond the film's own tight frame. I hope that this book similarly helps to open up the film for the reader, whether or not she agrees with the arguments and interpretations I have presented in these pages. There is a lot more to say about *Word Is Out*, its makers, and its participants, as well as about the many ways that the film has affected the course of gay and lesbian life and politics. I hope the conversations continue.

REFERENCES

Adair, Nancy. 1978. Nancy's story. In N. Adair and C. Adair 1978, 265–317.

Adair, Nancy, and Casey Adair, eds. 1978. *Word is out: Stories of some of our lives.* San Francisco: New Glide Publications.

Adair, Peter, Papers (GLC 70). The James C. Hormel Gay and Lesbian Center, San Francisco Public Library.

———. 1974. Coming out: A proposal for a gay film. In Adair Papers, box 33, folder 26.

———. 1978. Distributing *Word Is Out.* In Adair Papers, box 55, folder 15.

———. 1993. Peter Adair's speech presented to Artlink, October 2, 1993. Included in the press kit for the *Word Is Out* thirtieth-anniversary DVD release. http://www.wordisoutmovie.com/PressKit/WordIsOutPK.pdf

———. n.d. So you want to be a collective, or let's tie our shoelaces. Excerpted in the press kit for the *Word Is Out* thirtieth-anniversary DVD release. http://www.wordisoutmovie.com/PressKit/WordIsOutPK.pdf

Agamben, Giorgio. 1998. *Homo sacer: Sovereign power and bare life.* Stanford: Stanford University Press.

Arendt, Hannah. 1951. *The origins of totalitarianism.* Cleveland: Meridian Books.

Atwell, Lee. 1978. Review of *Word Is Out* and *Gay USA. Film Quarterly* 32 (2): 50–57.

Austin, J.L. 1976. *How to do things with words*, 2nd ed. Oxford: Oxford University Press.

Babuscio, Jack. 1978. The cinema of camp (a.k.a. camp and the gay sensibility). In *Camp: Queer aesthetics and the performing subject: A reader*, ed. Fabio Cleto, 117–35. Ann Arbor: University of Michigan Press, 1999.

Blaney, Darren. 2011. *The AIDS Show* broke the silence. *The Gay & Lesbian Review* 18 (2): 13–16.

Bronski, Michael. 1978. Review of *Word is Out: Stories of Some of Our Lives*. *Gay Community News*, April 29.

———. 2002. The real Harry Hay. *Boston Phoenix*, October 31.

Brown, Wendy. 1995. *States of injury: Power and freedom in late modernity*. Princeton: Princeton University Press.

Butts, Gavin. 2007. 'Stop that acting!': Performance and authenticity in Shirley Clarke's *Portrait of Jason*. In *Pop art and vernacular cultures*, ed. Kobena Mercer, 36–55. Cambridge: MIT Press.

Chasin, Alexandra. 2000. *Selling out: The gay and lesbian movement goes to market*. New York: Palgrave.

Clendinen, Dudley, and Adam Nagourney. 1999. *Out for good: The struggle to build a gay rights movement in America*. New York: Simon & Schuster.

Crimp, Douglas. 1987. How to have promiscuity in an epidemic. In *AIDS: Cultural analysis/cultural activism*, ed. Douglas Crimp, 237–71. Cambridge: MIT Press.

———. 2002. Mario Montez, for shame. In *Regarding Sedgwick: Essays on queer culture and critical theory*, eds. Stephen M. Barber and David L. Clark, 57–70. New York: Routledge.

Dangerous Bedfellows, eds. 1996. *Policing public sex*. Boston: South End Press.

D'Emilio, John. 1983. *Sexual politics, sexual communities: The making of a* homosexual minority in the United States, 1940–1970*. Chicago: University of Chicago Press.

Dunlap, David W. 1996. Obituary of Peter Adair. *New York Times*, June 30.

Dyer, Richard. 1990. *Now you see it: Studies on lesbian and gay film*. London: Routledge.

Echols, Alice. 1989. *Daring to be bad: Radical feminism in America, 1967–1975*. Minneapolis: University of Minnesota Press.

Epstein, Rob. 1981. *Word Is Out:* Stories of working together. *Jump Cut* 24/25: 9.

Erens, Patricia. 1988. Women's documentary: The personal is political. In Rosenthal 1988, 554–65.

Fejes, Fred. 2008. *Gay rights and moral panic: The origins of America's debate on homosexuality*. New York: Palgrave Macmillan.

Gearhart, Sally. 1978. *The wanderground: Stories of the hill women*. Watertown, Massachusetts: Persephone Press.

Gidlow, Elsa. 1986. *ELSA: I come with my songs*. San Francisco: Booklegger Press.

Gregg, Ron. 1992. PBS and AIDS. *Jump Cut* 37: 64–71.

Guthman, Edward. 1981. The way we are: Revisiting the *Word Is Out* folks. The *Advocate* (August 20): 36–40.

Hay, Harry. 1976. Gay liberation: Chapter two: Serving social/political change through our gay window: A position paper. In *Radically gay: Gay liberation in the words of its founder*, ed. Will Roscoe, 201–16. Boston: Beacon Press, 1996.

Hays, Matthew. 2007. *The view from here: Conversations with gay and lesbian filmmakers*. Vancouver: Arsenal Pulp Press.

Higgins, Ross. 2006. L'Apothéose d'Alan B. Stone et le retour d'Elsa Gidlow. *Archigai* 16: 3.

Holmlund, Chris, and Cynthia Fuchs, eds. 1997. *Between the sheets, in the streets: Queer, lesbian, gay documentary*. Minneapolis: University of Minnesota Press.

Iris Films. 1978. Iris Films interviewed: Lesbians lose their kids in custody cases. Interview by Cathy Cade, John Hess, and Carole Raimondi. *Jump Cut* 19: 6–8.

Jenkins, Philip. 1998. *Moral panic: Changing concepts of the child molester in modern America*. New Haven: Yale University Press.

Kahana, Jonathan. 2008. *Intelligence work: The politics of American documentary.* New York: Columbia University Press.

Kellner, Douglas, and Dan Streible, eds. 2000. *Emile de Antonio: A reader.* Minneapolis: University of Minnesota Press.

Kelly, Keith. 1979. The sexual politics of Rosa Von Praunheim. *Millennium Film Journal* 3: 115–18.

Kissack, Terence. 1995. Freaking fag revolutionaries: New York's Gay Liberation Front, 1969–1971. *Radical History Review* 62: 104–34.

Lesage, Julia. 1984. Feminist documentary: Aesthetics and politics. In *'Show us life': Towards a history and aesthetics of the committed documentary*, ed. Thomas Waugh, 223–51. Metuchen, New Jersey: The Scarecrow Press.

Levy, Dan. 2000. Ever the warrior: Gay rights icon Harry Hay has no patience for assimilation. *San Francisco Chronicle*, June 23.

Lorde, Audre. 1979. The master's tools will never dismantle the master's house. In *Sister outsider: Essays and speeches by Audre Lorde*, 110–13. Freedom, California: The Crossing Press, 1984.

Mariposa Film Group. 1977. Interview by Linda Artel. In Adair Papers, box 44, folder 14.

———. 1978. Interview by DuMont Howard and Jeffrey Escoffier. *Cineaste* 8 (4): 8–11, 59.

Marx, Karl. 1843. On the Jewish question. In *The Marx-Engels Reader*, ed. Robert C. Tucker, 26–52. 2nd ed. New York: Norton, 1978.

Maslin, Janet. 1978. Review of *Word Is Out: Stories of Some of Our Lives*. *New York Times*, March 26.

Muñoz, José Esteban. 2008. *Cruising utopia: The then and there of queer futurity*. New York: New York University Press.

Nichols, Bill. 1983. The voice of documentary. In Rosenthal 1988, 48–63.

———. 1992. *Representing reality: Issues and concepts in documentary*. Bloomington: Indiana University Press.

———. 1994. *Blurred boundaries: Questions of meaning in contemporary culture*. Bloomington: Indiana University Press.

Olson, Ray. 1979. Gay film work: Affecting but too evasive. *Jump Cut* 20: 9–12.

Rancière, Jacques. 2006. *Hatred of democracy*. London: Verso.

Redstockings, ed. 1975. *Feminist revolution*. New Paltz, N.Y.: Redstockings, Inc.

Rosenthal, Alan, ed. 1988. *New challenges for documentary*. Berkeley: University of California Press.

Russo, Vito. 1978. The interview ticket: *Word Is Out*. *The Advocate* (April 5): 30–31, 43.

Savage, Dan. 2011. Introduction. *It gets better*, eds. Dan Savage and Terry Miller. New York: Dutton.

Shilts, Randy. 1982. *The mayor of Castro Street: The life & times of Harvey Milk*. New York: St. Martin's Press.

Siegel, Marc. 1997. Documentary that dare/not speak its name: Jack Smith's *Flaming Creatures*. In Holmlund and Fuchs 1997, 91–106.

Stryker, Susan. 2008. *Transgender history*. Berkeley: Seal Press.

Terkel, Studs. 1974. *Working: People talk about what they do all day and how they feel about what they do*. New York: Pantheon Books.

Third World Gay Revolution. 1971. What we want, what we believe. In *Out of the closets: Voices of gay liberation*, eds. Karla Jay and Allen Young, 363–67. 20th-anniversary ed. New York: New York University Press, 1992.

Timmons, Stuart. 1990. *The trouble with Harry Hay*. Boston: Alyson Publications.

Waldman, Diane. 1978. There's more to a positive image than meets the eye. *Jump Cut* 18: 31–32.

Waugh, Thomas. 1976. Beyond vérité: Emile de Antonio and the new documentary of the 70s. *Jump Cut* 10/11: 33–39.

———. 1977. Films by gays, for gays: *Who Are We?*, *A Very Natural Thing*, *The Naked Civil Servant*. *Jump Cut* 16: 14–18. (A slightly revised version appears in Waugh 2000, 14–33.)

———. 1988. Lesbian and gay documentary: Minority self-imaging, oppositional film practice, and the question of image ethics. In *Image ethics: The moral rights of subjects in photographs, film, and television*, eds. Larry Gross, John Stuart Katz, and Jay Ruby, 248–72. New York: Oxford University Press.

———. 1997. Walking on tippy toes: Lesbian and gay liberation documentary of the post-Stonewall period, 1969–84. In Holmlund and

Fuchs 1997, 107–24. (A slightly revised version appears in Waugh 2000, 246–71.)

———. 2000. *The fruit machine: Twenty years of writings on queer cinema*. Durham, NC: Duke University Press.

Worth, Sol, and John Adair. 1972. *Through Navajo eyes: An exploration in film communication and anthropology*. Bloomington: Indiana University Press.

Žižek, Slavoj. 2007. Tolerance as an ideological category. *Critical Inquiry* 34 (4): 660–82.

FILMOGRAPHY

Absolutely Positive, Peter Adair, USA, 1991, 84 min.

The AIDS Show, Peter Adair and Robert Epstein, USA, 1986, 58 min.

Armee der Liebenden oder Revolte der Perversen (*Army of Lovers, or Revolt of the Perverts*), Rosa von Praunheim, West Germany, 1979, 95 min.

Le chagrin et la pitié (*The Sorrow and the Pity*), Marcel Ophüls, France, 1969, 260 min.

Common Threads, Robert Epstein and Jeffrey Friedman, USA, 1989, 79 min.

Gay USA, Arthur Bressan, USA, 1978, 78 min.

Gimme Shelter, Albert Maysles, David Maysles, and Charlotte Zwerin, USA, 1970, 91 min.

Growing Up Female, Julia Reichert and James Klein, USA, 1971, 50 min.

Hearts and Minds, Peter Davis, USA, 1974, 112 min.

Holy Ghost People, Peter Adair, USA, 1967, 52 min.

In the Best Interests of the Children, Iris Films (Frances Reid, Elizabeth Stevens, and Cathy Zheutlin), USA, 1977, 51 min.

Johan, Philippe Vallois, France, 1976, 85 min.

Looking for Langston, Isaac Julien, UK, 1989, 45 min.

One Flew Over the Cuckoo's Nest, Milos Forman, USA, 1975, 133 min.

Portrait of Jason, Shirley Clarke, USA, 1967, 98 min.

Screen Test #2, Andy Warhol and Ronald Tavel, USA, 1965, 66 min.

Sebastiane, Derek Jarman and Paul Humfress, UK, 1976, 85 min.

Some of Your Best Friends, Kenneth Robinson, USA, 1971, 39 min.

Superdyke, Barbara Hammer, USA, 1975, 17 min.

The Times of Harvey Milk, Robert Epstein, USA, 1984, 88 min.

Tongues Untied, Marlon Riggs, USA, 1989, 55 min.

Triumph des Willens (Triumph of the Will), Leni Riefenstahl, Germany, 1935, 120 min.

Underground, Emile de Antonio, Mary Lampson, and Haskell Wexler, USA, 1976, 88 min.

A Very Natural Thing, Christopher Larkin, USA, 1974, 85 min.

Winter Soldier, Winterfilm Collective, USA, 1972, 95 min.

The Woman's Film, San Francisco Newsreel, USA, 1971, 40 min.

Women I Love, Barbara Hammer, USA, 1976, 22 min.

Word Is Out: Stories of Some of Our Lives, Mariposa Film Group (Nancy Adair, Peter Adair, Andrew Brown, Robert Epstein, Lucy Massie Phenix, and Veronica Selver), USA, 1978, 132 min.

INDEX

Note: Page numbers for photographs in **bold**.

GREG YOUMANS is a scholar of queer activist and experimental filmmaking, with a particular interest in the 1970s. He received his PhD from the History of Consciousness program at the University of California, Santa Cruz. Youmans is currently at work on a larger book project entitled *Moral Panic Media: Gay and Lesbian Filmmaking in the Time of Anita Bryant*. He is also a film and video maker. In collaboration with Chris Vargas, he makes the ongoing video series *Falling in Love … with Chris and Greg*. Youmans lives in Oakland, California.

About the editors

MATTHEW HAYS is a Montreal-based critic, author, programmer, and university instructor. He has been a film critic and reporter for the weekly *Montreal Mirror* since 1993. His first book, *The View from Here: Conversations with Gay and Lesbian Filmmakers* (Arsenal Pulp Press), won a 2008 Lambda Literary Award. His articles have appeared in a broad range of publications, including *The Guardian, The Daily Beast, The Globe and Mail, The New York Times,* CBC Arts Online, *The Walrus, The Advocate, The Toronto Star, The International Herald Tribune, Cineaste, Cineaction, The Hollywood Reporter, Canadian Screenwriter, Xtra,* and *fab*. He teaches courses in journalism, communication studies, and film studies at Concordia University, where he received his MA in communication studies in 2000.

THOMAS WAUGH is the award-winning author of numerous books, including five for Arsenal Pulp Press: *Out/Lines, Lust Unearthed, Gay Art: A Historic Collection* (with Felix Lance Falkon), *Comin' at Ya!* (with David Chapman), and *Montreal Main: A Queer Film Classic* (with Jason Garrison). His other books include *Hard to Imagine, The Fruit Machine,* and *The Romance of Transgression in Canada*. He teaches film studies at Concordia University in Montreal, Canada, where he lives. He has taught and published widely on political discourses and sexual representation in film and video, on queer film and video, and has developed interdisciplinary research and teaching on AIDS. He is also the founder and coordinator of the program in Interdisciplinary Studies in Sexuality at Concordia.

Titles in the Queer Film Classics series: